Twayne's English Authors Series

EDITOR OF THIS VOLUME

Kinley E. Roby

Northeastern University

David Jones

TEAS 246

photograph: Julian Sheppard

David Jones

DAVID JONES

By SAMUEL REES

The University of Alberta

TWAYNE PUBLISHERS

A DIVISION OF G. K. HALL & CO., BOSTON

Copyright © 1978 by G. K. Hall & Co.

Published in 1978 by Twayne Publishers,
A Division of G. K. Hall & Co.
All Rights Reserved

Printed on permanent/durable acid-free paper and bound
in the United States of America

First Printing

Library of Congress Cataloging in Publication Data

Rees, Samuel, 1936–
David Jones.

(Twayne's English authors series ; TEAS 246)
Bibliography: p. 147–50
Includes index.
1. Jones, David Michael, 1895–1974—Criticism and interpretation.
PR6019.053Z86   1978   821'.9'12   78–9768
ISBN 0–8057–6726–6

Contents

About the Author

Preface

Chronology

1. Biographical   11

2. *Epoch and Artist*   34

3. *In Parenthesis*   49

4. *The Anathemata*   74

5. *The Sleeping Lord*   99

6. The Modern Context   121

    Notes and References   142

    Selected Bibliography   147

    Index   151

About the Author

Samuel Rees was born in Brazil of Welsh parents and raised and educated at Emmanuel Grammar School in Swansea, Wales. After emigration to the U.S. in 1953 and three years' service in the U.S. Marine Corps, he took a B.A. in English at San Diego State University and the M.A. and Ph.D. degrees at the University of Washington, Seattle. In 1969 he was appointed to the Department of English at the University of Alberta, Canada, where he is at present Associate Professor.

His special interests in modern poetry lie in the "Celtic Fringe," with particular attention to the work of Anglo-Welsh poets (R. S. Thomas, Dylan Thomas, Vernon Watkins, and David Jones); and in addition to articles in *The Anglo-Welsh Review*, *Albion*, and *Modern Poetry Studies* has recently published *David Jones: An Annotated Bibliography and Guide to Research* (Garland, 1977).

Preface

This study is intended to serve as an introduction to, and critical assessment of, the poetry and thought of David Jones. I should not take it amiss if scholars well versed in Jones should find in it something of value; however, the book is not written for the specialist and is given more to explanation and elucidation than probing critical analysis. Jones's is not simple poetry, easy of access, and I have attempted to treat it in a way that will not dishonor Jones either by simplifying him — i.e., minimizing or shrugging off the difficulties — or by consigning his achievement to the preserve of professional scholars and initiates.

I wish also, without apology, to advocate the reading and study of Jones's work. Not that he has been shockingly ignored, but that he is not yet as widely known or read as he should be; also that for reasons touching on the publishing history of his works and his apparent emergence too late from the "modernist" movement in poetry, it has been all too easy for some to dismiss him as an imitator. I am then at some pains to establish Jones's readability and worth in his own right.

Chapter 1 is largely biographical, since David Jones's work cannot be understood without careful attention to his roots in London and Wales, his service as a private in the 1914–1918 War, and his subscription to Roman Catholicism. Chapter 2 is a study of Jones's philosophy and aesthetics as set forth in the prose collection, *Epoch and Artist*; chapters 3 and 4 are close critical readings of his major long poems, *In Parenthesis* and *The Anathemata*. Chapter 5 is concerned with the shorter verse "fragments," most of which were not gathered together until 1974, the year of Jones's death, in *The Sleeping Lord: and other fragments*. In Chapter 6 I attempt to place and measure Jones among his contemporaries, specifically his fellow poet-combatants of the 1914-1918 War, his fellow Welshmen, and finally T. S. Eliot and James Joyce. Without, I hope, undermining my stated intention to be Jones's "advocate," Chapter 6 is the most clearly critical or judgmental.

Preface

While I do touch inevitably on Jones's work in other media — wood and copper engraving, watercolor, inscription — such attention forms no large part of this study for a number of reasons. First is the stated intention of this "authors" series; second is my conviction that Jones's importance lies primarily in his poetry; third, that his artwork does not lend itself to reduced reproduction and is not generally accessible in its originals to most readers, particularly those in North America; and fourth because it is discussed at some length, and very competently indeed, in David Blamires's *David Jones: Artist and Writer*.

A couple of personal notes: I have had occasion in the writing of this book to modify readings and judgments I have published previously. Following Kathleen Raine's "we do not so much change our minds as discover them," I have discovered, from discussions with other scholars, listening to their lectures, reading their published essays and reviews (and, of course, rereading David Jones many times over), some inadequacy in my earlier writings. These are not responsible, of course, for what might be judged continuing inadequacies, but my debt to the scholarship and enthusiasm of David Blamires (Manchester University), W. F. Blissett (The University of Toronto), and Jeremy Hooker (The University of Wales, Aberystwyth) goes far beyond merely listing their works in the bibliography.

I am pleased to acknowledge financial support I have received from the Canada Council during the preparation of this book, and would like further to express my appreciation for their hospitality and assistance to: Mr. David Jenkins, Librarian, The National Library of Wales, Aberystwyth; the National Museum of Wales, Cardiff; Professor C. J. L. Price and the University College of Swansea: the Woodberry Poetry Room of Lamont Library, Harvard University; the libraries of the University of Washington at Seattle, and Seattle University; and the library of St. Joseph's College and the Rutherford Library at the University of Alberta.

To the office staff of the University of Alberta's Department of English — with special mention of Linda Ziolkowski — go my thanks for their aid in preparation of the manuscript.

Acknowledgments

Quotations from David Jones's *In Parenthesis, The Anathemata, Epoch and Artist,* and *The Sleeping Lord: and other fragments* are reprinted by permission of Faber & Faber, Ltd.; quotations in poetry and prose from *Agenda* (Spring-Summer, 1967; Autumn-Winter, 1973 - 74; Winter-Spring, 1975), from *David Jones: Letters to Vernon Watkins,* ed. Ruth Pryor (University of Wales Press, 1976), from René Hague, *David Jones* (University of Wales Press, 1975), and from *David Jones: Eight Essays on His Work As Writer and Artist,* ed. Roland Mathias (Gomer Press, 1976), with acknowledgment to the authors, editors, and publishers, and by permission of The Trustees of the David Jones Estate. Quotations from T. S. Eliot, *Selected Essays* and *Four Quartets* are reprinted by permission of Faber & Faber, Ltd. and Harcourt Brace Jovanovich, Inc.; those from *The Cantos of Ezra Pound* by permission of Faber & Faber, Ltd. and New Directions Publishing Corp., New York; from Wilfred Owen, *Collected Poems,* ed. C. Day Lewis, by permission of the Owen Estate, Chatto and Windus, Ltd., and New Directions Publishing Corp., New York; from R. S. Thomas, *Selected Poems: 1946 - 1948* and *Song at the Year's Turning,* by permission of Hart-Davis MacGibbon, Ltd., Granada Publishing Ltd. Frontispiece photograph by Julian Sheppard, F.R.S.P.

Chronology

1895   Born November 1 in Brockley, Kent, third child of James and Alice Ann (Bradshaw) Jones.

1904   ("Or thereabouts") first visits paternal grandparents in North Wales.

1909–   Studies at the Camberwell School of Art.
1914

1915   January 2, enlists as a private in the 15th (London-Welsh) Battalion of the Royal Welsh Fusiliers; in December, embarks for France.

1916   July 10-11, wounded at Mametz Wood, the Battle of the Somme; October, returns to France after recuperation.

1918   Demobilized at Limerick, Ireland.

1919–   Studies at the Westminster School of Art; January 29, 1921,
1921   first meets Eric Gill; September 7, 1921, received as a convert to the Roman Catholic Church and adopts middle name "Michael."

1922–   January 1922, joins Eric Gill in the Guild of St. Joseph and
1926   St. Dominic at Ditchling, Sussex. Illustrates books for the St. Dominic Press. December 1924, visits Gill at Capel-y-Ffin, Wales; stays there and at Caldey Island, Pembrokeshire, frequently; illustrates publications of the Golden Cockerel Press.

1927–   Joins the Society of Wood Engravers; Spring 1928, travels
1934   with Gill to Salies de Béarn, France; lives variously at home at Brockley or in parents' bungalow at Portslade, Sussex. 1928, begins work on *In Parenthesis*. Frequent visitor with Gill at Pigotts, Buckinghamshire, at Caldey Island (last there in 1931), and at Helen Sutherland's residence, Rock Hall, Northumberland. Spring 1934, visits Egypt and Palestine with Gill.

1937   First edition of *In Parenthesis*.

1938   Receives the Hawthornden Prize for *In Parenthesis*.

1939   Moves to Pigotts; later to Sheffield Terrace, London.

1946   Moves to Harrow-on-the-Hill.

1952   First edition of *The Anathemata*.

1954   Receives the Russell Loines Award for *The Anathemata*.

1955   Awarded C. B. E. Publication of *Dock Leaves* (A David Jones Number).

1956   Receives the Harriet Monroe Memorial Prize for "The Wall."

1959   First edition of *Epoch and Artist*.

1960   Awarded honorary *D. Litt.* from the University of Wales, Aberystwyth.

1961   Made Fellow of the Royal Society of Literature; member of the Royal Water Colour Society. Receives Levinson Prize for "The Tutelar of the Place." New edition of *In Parenthesis* with "A Note of Introduction" by T. S. Eliot.

1962   Moves to Monksdene Residential Hotel, Harrow.

1964   "Foreword" and engravings (from 1929) for new edition of *The Rime of the Ancient Mariner*. Awarded Gold Medal for Fine Arts by the Royal National Eisteddfod of Wales.

1965   Publication of *The Fatigue* in honor of his seventieth birthday.

1967   Publication of *Agenda* (David Jones Special Issue).

1968   Awarded Midsummer Prize by the City of London.

1969   Publication in book form of *The Tribune's Visitation*; receives Honours Award of the Welsh Arts Council.

1972   "Word and Image" exhibition at the National Book League, London; publication of *Poetry Wales* (A David Jones Number); expanded "Introduction" to new edition of *The Rime of the Ancient Mariner*.

1973–   Publication of *Agenda* (David Jones Special Issue); June
1974   1974, made Companion of Honour in the Queen's Birthday Honours List. First edition of *The Sleeping Lord: and other fragments*; October 28, dies at Calvary Nursing Home, Harrow.

1975   Publication in book form of *The Kensington Mass*; founding of the David Jones Society.

CHAPTER 1

Biographical

I Introduction

DAVID Jones once schematized his life aptly and succinctly in characterizing himself as "a person whose perceptions are totally conditioned and limited by and dependent upon his being indigenous to this island"; and went on to describe himself, more specifically, as "a Londoner, of Welsh and English parentage, of Protestant upbringing, of Catholic subscription" (*A,** p. 11). Within that broad outline were to occur such biographical "accidents" as his prewar study at art school; his service as a private in the trenches in the 1914-1918 War; his further attendance at art school; his subsequent "apprenticeship," as it were, in the Dominican community at Ditchling led by Eric Gill; his lifelong bachelorhood. Never a hermit or solitary, still he was virtually "invisible"; his was a life of studied apartness but not disengagement; and he did not seek personal or literary or political reputation and fame. Jones did not write extensively of his own life, and if there is one word that is most inappropriate to describe his poetry, it is "confessional." In a short piece, "Autobiographical Talk," he wrote of his ancestral connections as being "accidental," and there exists in all his utterances on both his personal history and that of his whole culture an attitude which accepts the givens and preconditions of his own being in this time and place in history. It is a relentless self-effacement which stops, in Jones, far short of fatalism, and is accepted wholly in gratitude rather than in despair.

In the matter of Wales and his Welsh inheritance, he allowed, as if it had been decreed, the literature and mythology of the land of his father and his father's father to exercise perhaps the single most important influence on all aspects of his life and art. Similarly,

drawing, painting, and the visual arts he spoke of as another paren-
tal gift, traceable this time to his mother, of Italian-English extrac-
tion. Of his enlistment in the war, he wrote: "Here history came to
my aid and I found myself doing squad-drill with the Royal Welch
Fusiliers on the esplanade at Llandudno. I didn't much like that
either. Then there was France" (*E&A*, p. 28). The tone of passive
acceptance holds; the war was one of those historical accidents
which one has to endure. Today one is an art student; tomorrow he
finds himself in the ranks, then at the front, and there is little more
to be said about it. Well, there was *In Parenthesis* to be said about
it, but that poem is, literally, another story. Given the paternal
Welsh influence and the fact that Jones had been in the Teifi Valley
in Wales "trying to paint landscapes" at the time, however, there
seems little doubt that he found in the Royal Welch the only possible regiment with which to serve. Of his conversion, he described
how "sometime in 1917 somewhere in the neighbourhood of
Ypres... I first found myself wondering about the Catholic tradition. Four years later, in 1921, I found myself unable to do other
than subscribe to that tradition" (*E&A*, p. 28). He used the same
kind of language to describe his beginnings as a writer: "I found
myself trying my hand at the making of a writing" (*E&A*, p. 12).
Jones's language notwithstanding, it is important to note that in
choosing to become Roman Catholic he deliberately set aside the
faith of his fathers, and that his late achievement in the written
word as medium was the hard-won product of an individual act of
choice.

II   *The Early Life*

David Jones's origins were undistinguished, though the influence
of the "makers," the fabricators, in his family is significant. On his
father's side, the family was all Welsh, though of North Wales and
the Church of England. Jones was not a product of the chapel-
rugby-pub-coal-mine culture of industrial South Wales; had he
been so he would have been none the less Welsh, but of a distinctly
different strain. John Jones, his grandfather, was born at Ysceifiog
of farming stock and worked as plasterer in Holywell, Flintshire.
James Jones, son of Jones *Plastrwr,* was born in Treffynon in 1860
and raised in Gwynedd-is-Gonwy. After apprenticeship to a printer
in Holywell he went in the mid-1880s finally to London by way of
Liverpool. He was, his son wrote, "a Welshman of that generation

... whose parents were *determined* that he should be as English as possible. Consequently, he had only a rather feeble grasp of the Welsh language, knew virtually nothing of ancient Welsh tradition, but was deeply religious and, I *know*, 'felt' extremely 'Welsh.' "[1] In London, James Jones made a career as printer's overseer with the Christian Herald Publishing Company, and in 1888 married Alice Ann Bradshaw, age thirty-two.

She had been born in 1856 in Rotherhithe, Surrey, daughter of an English-Italian marriage; and it is in recognizing the influence of the maternal side of his family that the would-be "professional Welsh" advocate for Jones must give ground. Ebenezer Bradshaw, Alice's father, was an English mast-and-block maker, practicing his art (and I use the word deliberately) on the banks of the Thames at Rotherhithe. He died just before David, his grandson, was born, yet alone among members of the family he appears in Jones's written work, in *In Parenthesis* and in "Redriff" (an abbreviation for Rotherhithe), Part IV of *The Anathemata*. His influence is apparent too in Jones's lifelong preoccupation with the sea and ships as subjects and motifs in his painting and poetry. "Years later," Jones wrote, "in suburban Kent, I used to sit under a pear-tree on a small log of Ganges teak, brought there as an act of *pietas* by my parents along with some blocks and dead-eyes and other tackle and tools of ship's carpentry, just as reliques to recall the skilled artifex in his Thames-side yard."[2] Of more direct and personal influence, of course, was his mother, Alice Ann (Bradshaw) Jones. She was an amateur artist of some skill, though not of any public reputation. Her drawings were, Jones wrote, "in the manner of the Victorian drawing-master; not only competently but delicately and sensitively drawn" (*E&A*, p. 27). But most importantly she and her printer husband gave their third child encouragement in his drawing, and this nurtured talent led Jones to reminisce that by age six, deficient in all other lessons anyway, he had somewhere within him the assurance of a life dedicated to drawing.

David (Michael) Jones was born November 1, 1895, at Brockley, Kent, and grew up there in what was then a semirural atmosphere. ("Michael" is a name he took at the time of his acceptance into the Roman Catholic Church; he did not use it personally or professionally, though it is used frequently by bibliographers to distinguish him from other David Joneses — a not uncommon name.) Jones testified to an early childhood liking for the stories of Arthur and *The Lays of Ancient Rome* — as books to be read aloud to him: "I was very stupid in learning to read and found it hard at nine and subsequently. On more than one occasion I recall paying my sister a penny to read to me" (*A*, p. 41). His father read Bunyan aloud to him and also encouraged him in things Welsh — in English translation, however: "Even elementary French was beyond me, let alone mastering the extremely difficult language of my father's land."[3] David Jones was never to learn Welsh sufficiently to be fluent either orally or in the written language. "It is a pain of loss I must needs suffer,"[4] he once wrote, but no reader can accept Jones's judgment of himself that he was a "*dolt* at all languages."[5]

Jones wrote too of his first trip, as a boy of about seven, to Wales, and his sighting of high hills and sea together in one landscape: "I remember feeling some rubicon had been passed and that I was now in the land of which I had heard my father so often speak" (*E&A*, p. 27). In the figure of his grandfather, John Jones, he was to see a reincarnation from the Welsh legendary past.

He was, or, had been, a tall, powerful man, but now, like Llywarch Hen, his third foot was his staff. He was seated near the little stone oratory of St. Trillo on the sea-shore above the wattled sea-weir that was in those days still in use in Rhos and the vicar of Llandrillo was still entitled to his tithe of fish from that weir.

That wall of wattles and boulders set like a sheep-pen in the sea-channel, in the *camlas*, impressed me from my first sight of it and so did St. Trillo's chapel with its well of fresh water springing so near the salt sea-margin.

Once I knew the story of Taliesin I used consciously to associate this weir with Gwyddno's weir. And it may be that, earlier, my *un*conscious was making its *own* associations whereby my tall grandfather seated above the *cored* in Rhos may *possibly* have got mixed up with another figure in the Taliesin story, King Maelgwyn the Tall, who had his principal seat in Rhos. (*E&A*, p. 27)

Landscape and legend, fact and fiction, blurred as they often do for children; but with the young David Jones the blurring caught and remained for a lifetime. "Blurring" is perhaps not the best word; for Jones, the distinctness of detail as evidenced in this recollection is characteristic. "At all events," he added, "those visits in childhood showed to me visible and tangible survivals from a Welsh past in an, as yet, virtually unspoiled landscape. So that any subsequent interest in or musing upon that past was no doubt sustained and given body by a remembrance of those tokens that I saw on my happy visits to my relatives in North Wales" (*E&A*, p. 27).

"But it happened," Jones wrote to another Welsh poet, Vernon Watkins, in 1962, "that my bent was toward the visual arts,"[6] in which he received not only the encouragement of his parents but, in 1904, a prize from the Royal Drawing Society for "Dancing Bear," done at age seven — "There are few of my subsequent works which I prefer to that."[7] In his youth all his energy and talent were directed toward the visual arts, with no apparent hint that he would so concern himself as a writer in later life with "the full difficulty of somehow making viable the things of Wales in the only language I know, i.e. English."[8]

Jones's formal art training began at age fourteen at the Camberwell School of Art in 1909. To go there rather than have "Latin declensions and the elements of Greek knocked into me"[9] he had to plead to overcome his parents' initial objections; his mother's generosity to pavement artists did not imply that she thought it an ideal future for her son. There were required exercises in drawing from plaster casts of classic sculpture and life, but "it was still animals I most wanted to draw, still the cat-tribe and wolves and deer."[10] At Camberwell for four years he received the instruction of Reginald Savage and A. S. Hartrick, who, he testified, enabled him to be free from "the general dead weight of outside opinion"[11] and introduced him to the work of other artists — Gauguin, Van Gogh, the English Pre-Raphaelites, the Post-Impressionists, and others. In politics he considered himself a Lloyd George partisan and a committed London Welshman who thought he knew, but only vaguely, that he wanted to be an artist of some sort, perhaps one dealing with Welsh subjects.

III *The Soldier: 1914–1918*

The 1914-1918 War was to be a telling parenthesis in the education of the artist as a young man. Jones took with him finally (he was rejected on physical grounds — "insufficient chest expansion" — at first try at enlistment in 1914) his sketchbook and pencil and a mind and talent whose growth were severely aborted. The works he did in the war were, by his own account, of no consequence, "feeble impressionistic sketches such as might appear in any second-rate illustrated paper."[12] On January 2, 1915, he succeeded in joining the Royal Welsh Fusiliers, a regiment noted for its accumulated battle honors, and served as a private in the 38th (Welsh) Division, the 15th (London-Welsh) battalion. After training in

Llandudno, Wales, and Winchester, in December 1915 he embarked with the Division from Southampton to the shores of France. Robert Graves and Siegfried Sassoon were to be other notable writers serving in the same regiment, but Jones was to "know" them only many years later, through their books. Besides, they were officers.

Jones was not a successful soldier; he was, in his own words, "not only amateur, but grotesquely incompetent, a knocker-over of piles, a parade's despair" (*IP*, p. xv). These qualities did not, of course, prevent him from seeing action at the front, where on July 10-11, 1916, in Mametz Wood at the Battle of the Somme, he was wounded. It is this period of some seven months, from early December 1915 to early July 1916, that is treated in *In Parenthesis*. His companions were mostly Londoners and Welshmen, Cockneys and Taffys, who "bore in their bodies the genuine tradition of the Island of Britain," Jones was to note later in his preface to *In Parenthesis* (p. x); it was a time in which, before the devastation of this monstrously ill-advised and ill-carried-out battle, there was "a certain attractive amateurishness, and elbow-room for idiosyncrasy that connected one with a less exacting past" (*IP*, p. ix). The wounding of Private Ball occurs in Part VII of *In Parenthesis*; much later Jones was to give a nonfictionalized account of the incident:

Talking of "mass" and what the scientists tell us of velocity causing weight — I suppose that's why when a machine-gun or maybe rifle bullet passed clean through my left leg without touching the fibula or tibia — but merely through the calf, it felt as if a great baulk of timber or a heavy bar of some sort had struck me sideways, in fact I thought a ponderous branch had been severed by shrapnel and had fallen across my leg but couldn't account for the *extreme violence and weight*. I did not realize it was S.A.A. until I tried to stand up & felt the wetness seeping from the wound that I'd been hit by a mere little bullet, but the disproportion of the smallness of the nickel projectile and the great bludgeoning weight of the impact astonished me even at the time.[13]

The dispassionate and decidedly non-self-pitying account in Jones's own words is characteristic; the greater truth of the matter is to be found in the poem, which too, however, will be without the pity of it. The sequel, a time of confusion in the woods, is also a part of *In Parenthesis* which bears comparison with Jones's account in a letter to René Hague:

...after a bit more crawling I found I should have to abandon it [my rifle], which I did, still with a sense of shame & a feeling that can only be described as real affection.... Looking at a corporal whom I recognised as of my own battalion — I did not know him at all well but I can see his kindly Welsh face — a countryman's face, but I recall only his lifting me up and carrying me on his back. We had not got far when in the darkness or half darkness a tall figure emerged who happened to be a Major.... He said "is that you Corporal X?" "Yes, I was trying to carry Pte Jones a bit nearer the advance dressing station or find some stretcher bearers Sir." "Corporal X, you will no matter *who* he is, drop the bugger *here*. If every wounded man is to be carried from where he has chanced to fall, by a corporal or any other of the rank and file, we would double our loss of fire-strength & that's not over-much as it is. Put Pte Jones (of 'B', I think?) down immediately. Stretcher-bearers will find him within a short time. Don't you know there's a sod of a war on."[14]

Jones was evacuated to England and treated in Warwickshire, but returned to another front in late October 1916. Less vulnerable physically in the new posting, perhaps, he recorded a distaste for the assignment: "I can only register a very considerable change of feelings and conditions.... The increased use of mechanical transport, and mechanization in general, made the whole 'feel' very different from the war I had known in the months before the Somme battle."[15]

The full extent to which *In Parenthesis* is autobiographical will have to await examination of the collection of Jones's correspondence and private papers. However, "Parts 3 & 4 are virtually a pretty exact chronicle. Part 5 uses remembered things as 'materia poetica' covering a number of months from say January 1916 to May or June 1916.... Anyway Part 5 has nothing in it that was not actually experienced, but unlike most of the other parts telescopes the routine...etc."[16] One other incident recorded in *In Parenthesis*, Private Ball's observation of a gentle French priest who "walked between his vegetable beds; he handled his small black book as children do their favourite dolls, who would impute to them a certain personality" (*IP*, p. 117), likely marks the time, redated in poetic fiction, when Jones first felt some leanings toward the Catholic church. (Robert Graves, convalescing in the Isle of Wright, made friends with French Benedictines in a nearby abbey and wrote: "At Quarr, Catholicism ceased to repel me.")[17]

Early in 1918, "January or February," he became severely ill with trench-fever and was sent back to England, thus missing, in his words, "the astonishing German offensives of March and

April."[18] Eventually, in August, he was sent to Limerick, Ireland, to await demobilization after the Armistice. The parenthesis was closed, but its effects were to linger in his art and in his physical and psychological life; he was never able to say, with Robert Graves, "goodbye to all that." He wrote: "As far as I am able to judge my own case I should say that the particular Waste Land that was the forward area of the West Front had a permanent effect on me and has affected my work in all sorts of ways" (*E&A*, p. 28). In another mention of what it was to be at the front, Jones shifted to talk of "them," his Welsh and English companions: "...for I think the day by day in the Waste Land, the sudden violences and the long stillnesses, the sharp contours and unformed voids of that mysterious existence, profoundly affected the imaginations of those who suffered it" (*IP*, p. 10). The war experience was not to be exorcised in his art, and he never entertained the view that art was in any way therapeutic. But of his nervous breakdowns, some three or four in his lifetime, he noted: "It is impossible to talk of these things, of the complete relapse into fear, of incapacity.... But they have cut my production in half."[19]

While the war years represented truly a traumatic parenthesis for Jones, a block of time wrenched from his continued study in art, they made finally for his poetry a fortuitous parenthesis. More of real worth for Jones's subsequent writings has its beginnings in the 1914-1918 War than was ever to appear in his visual art. The experience of the war clearly could find no outlet in his paintings, which are generally of a still, even pastoral quality, or of a distant, nervously executed, tapestried design. Jones himself felt that the hundreds of trench sketches that he made were of no value whatsoever, and it is only his illustrations published in *In Parenthesis* which reflect visually that war at all. Yet the institution, the camaraderie, the absurdity, the savageness, the human ritual, the "sacrament" of war permeate and charge all his writings.

IV   *Postwar Years: Conversion and Apprenticeship*

In 1919 Jones resumed formal art-school training, this time on a government grant at the Westminster School of Art. Under Headmaster Walter Bayes (who was later to encourage him to join Eric Gill at Ditchling) and in Bernard Meninsky's life-classes, Jones studied the basics — the uses of materials, media, the painter's tools, the techniques. He began to learn the true vocation of the artist, beginning with recognition of the primary importance of painstaking dedication to mastery of his art and craft; here was neither rigid, imitative formalism nor abandoned expressionism. All his subsequent work in every medium evidences the utmost devotion to detail and care for the craft of making a work of art, whether visual or written. At this time Jones was particularly enthusiastic about the works of Blake, a fellow painter, engraver, and poet with whom he has often been compared.

On January 29, 1921, Jones met Eric Gill at Ditchling, Sussex, their introduction arranged by Father John O'Connor (the putative Father Brown of G. K. Chesterton's detective stories), who was later to receive Jones into the Church. Jones went as a curious visitor but also as one who was floundering, who had jaded views on "the futility of all art-school training"[20] and needed new direction in his art and life.

It was a very wet day, and he found Eric in his workshop. Eric went on working and presently said: "You don't have a very clear idea of the direction you're going in, do you?" Jones agreed that he did not. Then Eric took a piece of paper and drew a roughly triangular figure with the corners not meeting, followed by a second in which they nearly met but not quite, and finally a third where they met perfectly.

"Which of those do you think is a triangle?" he asked. Jones replied that he did not know, but that he liked one of them better than the others.

"It's not a question of being better," said Eric; "the other two aren't triangles at all."[21]

Jones went home, but on September 7 of the same year he completed the step he had first contemplated in France in 1917, and in Bradford, under the guidance of Father O'Connor, joined the Roman Catholic Church. Gill knew about the conversion, and it was only six days later that he wrote to Father O'Connor: "We are delighted about David, and hope he'll come back before long (then we'll have to keep him up to the mark and knock some corners off him D.V.)."[22] For Jones, the move to Rome seems to have come about not through deep psychic struggle, not through pangs of conscience or intense sense of personal need, but through aesthetic theory. It was deep intellectual curiosity and critical investigation of the origins and continuing meaning of the arts, rather than concern for the soul or eternity, which brought Jones to his decision. He described the process in an essay written much later:

When, in 1919, I re-commenced by studies as an art-student, my fellow-students and I wasted a good deal of our time (I hope art-students are still so occupied) discussing, not without heat, the "nature of art." As the opinion "There's nothing like leather" was our opinion also, we meant by "art" the arts of painting, sculpture, etc. For one reason or another certain queries touching what Christians did or did not assert with regard to the eucharist were at that time much in my mind, and though I in no way connected these queries with the queries concerning the arts, I sometimes found myself thinking of the two matters together, though still unrelatedly. The question of analogy seemed not to occur until certain Post-Impressionist theories began to bulk larger in our student conversation. Then, with relative suddenness, the analogy between what we called "the Arts" and the things that Christians called the eucharistic signs became (if still but vaguely) apparent (*E&A*, p. 171).

The importance of his shift to Roman Catholicism (it can scarely be called a conversion, certainly not in the apocalyptic Saul-on-the-road-to-Damascus sense) can scarcely be overstated, though T. S. Eliot's comment on Gerald Manley Hopkins's conversion is pertinent and worth repeating: "To be converted, in any case, while it is sufficient for entertaining the hope of individual salvation, is not going to do for a man, as a writer, what his ancestry and his country for some generations back have failed to do."[23] It might be, in Jones's case, that his Catholicism is secondary to his Welshness, though the two are mutually complementary and integrated wholly in his art. All of Jones's life and work was to be directed to the fulfilling of his vision of Catholic ideas in art; his poetry, particularly that following *In Parenthesis,* is a tenacious and dedicated affirmation of his Catholic subscription.

In November 1921 Jones left London and the Westminster School of Art and joined Eric Gill (who was himself a convert to the Church) at Ditchling Common, Sussex, in the Guild of St. Joseph and St. Dominic. While he lived in the community for four years, he was never actually a member of the guild, which was a working group of Catholic craftsmen-artists and their families and apprentices. It was a nonutopian, nonmonastic organization, a working and prospering brotherhood bonded by devotion to art and the Church, and laboring daily, both in works of art within and without the Ditchling community and in formal devotions, to glorify both muses. Here as apprentice Jones learned wood engraving from his mentors, chiefly Gill and Father Desmond Chute. "I think we can keep him employed and for myself," Gill wrote, "I promise you that I will do my best to see that he gets from us normal and 'no new-fangled popery.' "[24] George Maxwell tried to teach Jones carpentry — and Jones tried to learn — but to no avail; he evidently did not inherit Ebenezer Bradshaw's skills. The phrase "carpentry of song" to describe the poetry of the Welsh bards proved a happy image for Jones in formulating his ideas on the construction of a piece of writing, however. But he learned his engraving well, and was later to provide masterful copper and wood engravings and woodcut illustrations for finely produced editions of *The Rime of the Ancient Mariner* and *Gulliver's Travels.* Compared with Gill's work, however, Jones's delicate lines appear formal, stilted, and remote; his work is accomplished and interesting, but he seems not to have absorbed the sensuous vigor and versatility that is so characteristic of Gill. Even Gill's *Stations of the Cross* sculpture, with which Jones helped him, is wooden in comparison with the robust primitivism of some of Gill's other figures, mostly female, and the frequent mother-with-child sculptures.

For the next fifteen years Jones was to see much of Gill, though they were men of quite different temperaments — Gill the boisterous and often cantankerous leader of men, self-consciously a prophet, controversialist, and leader of movements; Jones, the already slightly withdrawn ascetic. In addition to his medieval-style religious work, Gill made illustrations for *Lady Chatterley's Lover*; Jones never wavered very far from the miracle plays and acceptable "classics." Yet they collaborated occasionally with happy results: "St. Michael as well as St. George appeared on the cross at Trumpinton, near Cambridge, with other panels representing the Blessed Virgin and Child beside the manger, and a foot-slogging soldier suggested by David Jones."[25] Jones acknowledged indebtedness to Gill not only as a friend but for "fruitful conversations.... He possessed...a Socratic quality, which, even in disagreement, tended to clarification" (*A*, p. 29). And in a rare effusive moment he added: "What a wonderful phase of one's life that Ditchling period was! When I think what I owe directly to Eric and then what I owe *indirectly* to him it amounts to an enormous debt. What an inimitable man he was."[26]

The Ditchling experiment attracted many visitors and much publicity; it suffered internal stresses, financial strains, quarrels among its participants, particularly Gill and Hilary Pepler, and on August 13, 1924, Gill and his family left. Breaches in the community were healed in part, however, according to Jones in a letter of the same date addressed to Desmond Chute: "Eric and the others departed this morning — leaving, what seems at the moment, a very desolate Ditchling. Moreover, you will be pleased to hear that any breach of friendship that may have existed was bridged before the departure — and charity rules the situation."[27] Jones himself left shortly thereafter, only to rejoin Gill in December of the same year, "without any initiative on my part" (*E&A*, p. 28), this time on what would seem for Jones very hospitable ground, Capel-y-Ffin in the Ewyas Valley of the Black Mountains of Wales. The Capel-y-Ffin move was to prove unsatisfactory to Gill, however; the site was too remote, too distant from sources of workable stone and markets, the living conditions too monastic and severe for the women. But Jones seems to have been happy; he was actively engaged as an engraver for the Golden Cockerel Press, which Robert Gibbings had acquired in 1924, and for which he illustrated *The Book of Jonah* (1926) and *The Chester Play of the Deluge* (1927). He made two long visits, the last in 1931, to an even more remote site, Caldey Island (Ynys Byr) off the coast at Pembrokeshire, working in the Scriptorium of a Benedictine establishment there.

Gill referred to David Jones as one with "a definite trade and a definite vocation to that trade"[28] which prevented him from going the way of another "stray sheep" in the Caldey community. In the next year, 1925, he was worrying about Jones at Caldey: "I don't know what'll happen to him. He's so determined to earn his living off his own bat — but he's so incapacitated by his temperament and unworkmanlike training."[29]

The effect of working in the Welsh environment on him was noted by Jones himself: "It was in the Black Mountains that I made some drawings which it so happens, appear, in retrospect, to have marked a new beginning. I began at this time to see the direction in which I wished to go — or at least to see it more clearly. My subsequent work can, I think, be truthfully said to hinge on that period. All my exhibited work dates from after that period, none or virtually none, from before it" (*E&A* p. 28). Thus it is from the mid-1920s, and more directly from the influence of Eric Gill and applied art, the aesthetics and philosophy of Jacques Maritain and the Roman Catholic Church, and the "strong hill-rhythms and the bright counter-rhythms of the *afonydd dyfroedd* of Nant Honddu" (*E&A,* p. 30) in Wales that Jones's emergence as an artist, as distinguished from an art student, can be dated. Some thirty-five years later Jones was to recall, and to savor the recollection and all its mythic and symbolic implications for the moment and for the future, when, "in Wales, the water supply of the house in which I was staying, was, on Christmas Eve, diverted at the source, which made it necessary for my friend, Mr. René Hague, and myself to go by night to where the mountain stream was deliberately blocked and to free the water. On our return journey Mr. Hague remarked, *'Duo homines per aquam nobis restituerunt rem'* " (*A*, p. 238). The line is a variation on Virgil, who borrowed it from Ennius, but its meaning and significance for Jones is its relation to the freeing of the waters by the god-hero to replenish the wasted land.

V   *The Artist*

The period from 1927 to 1933 was one of great activity for Jones. The year 1926 had seen him suffer the first of the breakdowns that afflicted him in his lifetime; a second was to occur in 1932, a year in which he produced fifty paintings. Back in London now, living with his parents in Brockley, Kent, and sometimes staying with them in their Portslade, Sussex, seaside bungalow, he painted a series of window seascapes: "I painted all the time; I never seemed to stop painting in those days."[30] He joined the Society of Wood Engravers in 1927 and had his first exhibition at St. George's Gallery of drawings done in Wales and at Hove. He was a regular visitor to Eric Gill and family at Pigott's in Buckinghamshire and Helen Sutherland at Rock, Northumberland; and in April 1928 he traveled with Gill to Salies de Béarn, Chartres, and Lourdes. The only reference that Gill makes to Jones by name in his *Autobiography* recalls this journey: "On one occasion I remember arguing, or what not, nearly all the night with David Jones and that helped us through the journey — much to the annoyance, I fear, of our fellow travelers who wished to sleep — but how absurd of them!"[31] Another observer noted that Gill's arguments with David Jones rarely "ran the risk of recrimination," though Gill "was once extremely angry with David Jones because he confessed to a certain distaste for apples. Apples were good; *ergo*, how could a rational man dislike them?"[32] Watercolors Jones made during this journey were exhibited at Goupil Gallery in 1928. Heal's Mansard Gallery displayed Jones's animal drawings, many done at the London Zoo, in 1930, and as a member of "The Seven and Five Society" Jones exhibited frequently from 1930 to 1933. The "7 and 5," as it came to be called, included Ben Nicholson, Ivon Hutchens, Barbara

Hepworth, Henry Moore, and others, and was set up to counter the "Bloomsbury" and "London Group" domination of the art scene. For his part, Jones claimed to have been "in a somewhat peripheral position to the major movements" of the 1930s, and cited his "antipathy to groups with stated aims."[33]

In 1934 he joined Eric Gill for a few months in Palestine, a voyage that was for Jones partly pilgrimage, mostly convalescence. It was, he wrote, a visit "forced because of illness," but went on to note that not only *The Anathemata* but virtually all of the Roman "fragments" had their origins in that experience.[34] And until the end of the decade he remained an itinerant, welcome for extended stays wherever he went — Sidmouth, Pigott's, Rock Hall, his parents' home, or Campion Hall, Oxford, with Father Martin C. D'Arcy, S.J., reputed to be "the smartest and most high-powered converting priest of them all."[35] In 1933 Jones's work was exhibited in the Chicago Exhibition, and in 1934 at the Venice Biennial International Exhibition of the Fine Arts. His reputation as an engraver and watercolorist was clearly widening, though it was not until the 1940s and 1950s that Jones's work was the subject for major exhibitions and one-man retrospectives at major galleries. Meanwhile, private collectors, notably Miss Helen Sutherland, and the Contemporary Art Society were buying his paintings.

But beginning in 1927 and 1928 Jones began to turn his attention to written art, overcoming the initial criticism of his father that it was a waste of time. He was never to forsake the visual arts, which he continued to practice throughout his life, but it seems increasingly clear that Jones's major achievement will be seen in the future to be his poetry. It is clear, too, that while Jones makes no qualitative distinctions between the various forms of art — all are equally worthy in the eyes of God; all must be the product of painstaking craftsmanship; all are those gratuitous, sacramental offerings of man's labor to his Maker — he was able to make statements in prose and poetry that his paintings and drawings, excellent as they are, complement, but seem unable quite to make for themselves. His watercolors evince a shimmering, nervous quality that keeps them delicately poised in space and time; outdoors merges with flowers in a vase in a window setting and each seems to blend into the other (*English Window* and *Manawyddan's Glass Door*). The washed colors spread over the squiggled pencil and pen lines which only temporarily and hesitatingly, it seems, are able to define forms, objects, outlines. Jones's animals (*Lynx* and *Panthers in*

Regents Park Zoo) have a remote, prehistoric look of restrained restlessness, of lithe strength and latent, subdued ferocity; the figures in his portraits — *Ladies at Mass, The Gladiator, Human Being, Petra im Rosenhag* — have a bleakly pensive, at once faraway and introspective, look. But no one painting, or for that matter all his paintings taken together, can convey the ideas contained in one thousand of his well-chosen words, not even such important and acclaimed Arthurian and "mythic" works as *Guenever and the Four Queens* and *Aphrodite in Aulis* of the early 1940s and *Trystan ac Esyllt*. It seems that Jones, by now an avid reader, particularly of Christopher Dawson and Jacques Maritain on Catholic theology and of Hopkins, Joyce, and Eliot as practicing poets, felt the inadequacies, despite the best preparation in his chosen vocation, of the visual media or his mastery of them.

Intellectually Jones was still wrestling, in the late 1920s and early 1930s, with what he and his friends christened "The Break," which bears some resemblance to what Eliot described as "dissociation of sensibility" but is concerned more immediately and specifically with the problem of the Christian artist who is working "outside a reasonably static culture-phase." That is, he is no longer sure of the recognizability or validity of his "signs," and in his use of the received language or "dogma" of the Church is left increasingly isolated and apparently irrelevant. It was not a matter of renouncing or rejecting that inheritance, however; Jones's inherent Catholic conservatism was, and is, evident: "...dogma concerning 'The Sacraments,' " he wrote, "...was taken by us for granted — was indeed our point of departure" (*A*, p. 16). And this was the postwar age of belligerent Fascism and Marxism, of lingering Bloomsbury, Surrealism, Cubism, etc., "isms" and movements and revolutions which Jones shunned utterly. For it was the repairing of "The Break," or rather the bridging of it, to satisfy man's "ineradicable longings for...the farther shore" (*A*, p. 16), that occupied Jones's attention. So far as art and religion were concerned Jones did achieve assurance, as the following letter, written much later, indicates. (The applicability of theory to the actual "making of a writing" had yet to be tested, however.)

From the doctrinal definition of the substantial presence in The Sacramental Bread, I learnt by an analogy, which could not in any way be pressed, that a tree in a painting or a tree in an embroidery must not be a re-presenting only of a tree, of sap and thrusting wood; it must really be a "tree," under the species of paint or needlework or whatever.... Certain ideas explicit or implicit in Catholic dogma had a clarifying and a considerably liberating effect. The Catholic Church's insistence on the reality of matter and spirit, that both are real and both good, acts obliquely in the most surprising connections. It weds form and content, and demands that in each particular the general should shine out, and that without the particular there could be no general for us men, and most important of all is The Church's assertion, against the moralists, that God made and maintains everything gratuitously. It is, similarly, this gratuitous quality, its less or greater presence, that makes a painting good or bad.... This "thingness" of a painting has been my sheet-anchor in times of bewilderment, that is, at all times.[36]

VI   The "Making of a Writing"

Thus we come to 1937 and to *In Parenthesis*, in work for ten years, the immediate subject of which is the Great War of 1914-1918, though it reaches back, as Jones emphasized so often, to a much older order.

In turning to the written word, as in his turn to the Catholic Church, Jones seems to have escaped the predetermined pattern of his life to that time; it was a decision made in maturity, albeit a time of nervous and physical strain, and not in impressionable youth. There is still, however, the disclaimer, "I found myself..." that he used in describing all the major turns and events in his life. The book has as its immediate subject the parenthesis of the years 1914-1918, or, more specifically, the period of December 1915 to July 1916. Yet another category of parenthesis is "our curious type of existence here" (*IP*, p. xv), he added. Another personal parenthesis worth noting is that of the years 1926 to 1932, a period opened and closed by physical and mental breakdowns and enclosing both a high period of creative achievement in the visual arts and a growing sense in Jones that his powers as a painter and engraver would not suffice. It was time for a new voice, a new medium, and it was to be poetry.

Jones had read extensively in the period between the wars, and noted particularly a "debt to conversations with and reading the books of Christopher Dawson."[37] He dated his interest in myth and the psychic past of man as beginning before Eliot's *The Waste Land*, and mentions reading Jessie Weston's *From Ritual to Romance* and Frazer's *The Golden Bough*, major sources in Eliot. His preparation for epic-writing, if a poet can be said, pointedly, to prepare for that, was slight, though he had read, while an art student, the right poets for that sort of effort — Chaucer, Malory,

Shakespeare, Milton — and he had come to know Celtic and Nordic literature in translation. Of contemporary poets he knew little except for the poems of T. S. Eliot, including Eliot's translation of St. John Perse's *Anabasis*. "I remember when I read *The Waste Land*. I thought, 'Now this has really said it, this has done it,' "[38] he told one interviewer. He had heard a recording by Joyce of what was to be part of *Finnegans Wake* — the "Anna Livia Plurabelle" section — and had read Gerard Manley Hopkins in 1928. But of the "war poets" he knew virtually nothing: "By 1928 I had read a good many 'war novels' but *extremely little* 'war poetry,' "[39] and he was not satisfied with the accounts of the war he had read except for Herbert Read's. At Ditchling he had not written verse, as had Eric Gill, Desmond Chute, and Hilary Pepler. Yet in 1937 he presented to T. S. Eliot and Faber & Faber a manuscript which earned immediate praise, won a major literary prize, and has received continuing literary acclaim.

Eliot, in a note of introduction for a 1961 reprinting, was to write: "*In Parenthesis* was first published in London in 1937. I am proud to share the responsibility for that first publication. On reading the book in typescript I was deeply moved. I then regarded it, and I still regard it, as a work of genius" (*IP,* p. vii). In Jones's words: "Tom Eliot . . . in those days was one of the governing chaps at Faber's and he insisted that they publish it."[40] The book received very favorable reviews, but it came too late, far too long after public awareness of the past war had dimmed, to allow it to sell very many copies. In form and style it was odd and demanding — now prose narrative, now "free" verse; now straightforward and clear, now allusive and esoteric. Herbert Read described Jones as a "Malory of the trenches,"[41] high praise accurately given, and *In Parenthesis* won the Hawthornden Prize in 1938. From subsequent reprintings in hardcover and in paperback it was to draw further critical acclaim, and today it is clear that the poem has confirmed the judgments of its first readers and survives as a classic of the literature of the 1914-1918 War.

VII   *1937 to 1952*

It was not to be long, of course, before another, even more devastating war was to rock Europe, and while the particular folly of the trenches was not to be repeated, the larger folly persisted. David Jones was forty-three in August 1939 at the time of Britain's declaration of war against Germany, and fit only to be a spectator, albeit a spectator likely both horrified and weary of it all. Some of the lingering sense of frustration is voiced in a verse fragment begun and abandoned in 1938, and not reworked finally for publication until 1966. *"A, a, a, Domine Deus"* voices a cry that is close to despair, a cry to God from one who knew only too well that "it is easy to miss Him / at the turn of a civilization." The psychic wounds of the previous war remain, and the poet despairs of ever seeing "the Living God projected from the Machine."

On September 5, 1939, Jones arrived at Pigott's with four refugee children, but instead of seeking pastoral retreats himself, he chose to remain in London close to his aging father. In one sense Jones escaped World War II; it could hold no new terrors for him. It does not appear as a theme or setting for his subsequent work, though *The Anathemata*, published in 1952 and in some respects to be seen as the musings of a Welsh-English Roman Catholic upon the Mass during World War II, makes slight allusion to it.

Discussing that poem and whether or not it had a "coherent shape, except that its end returned to its begining," Jones wrote that

We have to go back to the years of the Second World War—1938 or '9 was it, to whenever it closed — in the 1940s — I can't remember. Anyway, during the years of "Hitler's War" I had reason to be in London . . . and while there concentrated on writing a thing tentatively begun in 1937 . . . well, it would be truer to say that was the beginning of a new work altogether. Yes, definitely or completely new, really.[42]

So the years 1939 to 1945 were neither a parenthesis nor a hiatus. The year 1941 saw two major paintings, *Guenever and the Four Queens* and *Aphrodite in Aulis*, and Jones's fertile mind was gathering material for later works of pen and brush; he was shoring up the fragments of his life and times. He was anxious for his father in a London rest home (he died during the war), and anxious too in fear that Britain would be invaded. He was in bed with what appeared to be appendicitis for several weeks, and in 1947 "had a return of my 1932 breakdown, only much worse."[43] But this particular war, as a unique event in its own right, does not loom large in Jones's subsequent writings; to one who was a veteran of the trenches in 1914-1918 and who was immersed in history and antiquity to the extent that Jones always had been and was coming increasingly to be, it presented no new terror or insight.

It is worth noting that on May 30, 1941, *The Times* printed a letter written by Jones and a friend, the first of a number of letters by Jones on a variety of subjects that that newspaper chose to publish over the years. This letter displays an evident good humor, also evidence that Jones was not as wholly apolitical as he sometimes appears. It is a genteel conservatism attached both to the preservation of art (King Charles I's statue) and to the preservation of Royalist ideals that informs the mild protest. The cowriters considered the statue to be the "best post-medieval statue in London — indeed, the only true sensitive public statue in the capital"; but went further to hold that "another, if less pure reason might be urged: the nobility of the form happens to correspond with something in the content — it is the effigy of a man who was liquidated because of his attachment to a complex of many ancient and some gracious things, in face of the realities and inevitable ruthlessness of a military dictatorship and the necessities of a changing order."

Following his postwar breakdown and treatment (he was on many occasions to give thanks to those practitioners of the arts of medicine who enabled him to continue practicing his art), Jones took a room near the hospital at Northwick Lodge in Harrow-on-the-Hill. "I meant to stay a month or so, but actually stayed there for about fifteen years."[44] He was to live in and around Harrow, just outside London, for the rest of his life.

VIII *The Later Years*

In 1952 Jones was persuaded by Faber & Faber to publish *The Anathemata*, which he subtitled "fragments of an attempted writing." He wrote further in the preface of the poem's origins: "It had its beginning in experiments made from time to time between 1938 and 1945.... What is now printed represents parts, dislocated attempts, reshuffled and again rewritten intermittently between 1946 and 1951" (*A*, pp. 14-15). In apparatus — preface, footnotes, glossing — it outdoes *In Parenthesis*; thematically it is of wider scope, concerned with no less than the cultural and spiritual history of Western man. In form and technique the poem is rich, free, erudite, organic, allusive, and sometimes exasperating. Reviewers found much to praise, particularly the richness and virtuosity of the language, and in the contents, very often that which they could not understand but stood in awe of. Some had legitimate criticisms; others sneered at what they could not or did not want to comprehend. Auden, Kathleen Raine, W. F. Jackson Knight, among others, found much that was praiseworthy, both in the poem itself and in the long preface. Others, notably Edwin Muir, Hugh Kenner, and Howard Nemerov, had reservations, most often about the paraphernalia. The poem was reviewed widely, in the popular press, in Catholic literary circles, and in university quarterlies. Its publication revived interest in David Jones, of whom no one in literature had heard much for fifteen years. It did not, however, create for itself and its author a wide reading public, and after a decent interval it was largely forgotten. Among a small circle of initiates Jones's talent was appreciated, but he still had received little attention in the scholarly world, certainly nothing that would match the recognition he had received earlier as a painter. That oversight was to be remedied, at least in part, in the years remaining.

In 1954 *The Anathemata* was awarded the Russell Loines Memorial Award for poetry from the American National Institute of Arts and Letters, Jones being the first European recipient of the award since its inception in 1931. (The poem was not published in the United States until 1963, however.) Jones was made C.B.E. in 1955, and in 1968 received a major prize awarded by the Corporation of London to "the artist, writer, man of letters or science, who has made a major contribution to British cultural heritage, but who has received little recompense for his or her work."[45] In 1960 the University of Wales (Aberystwyth) granted him an honorary *D. Litt.*; the Welsh Committee of the Arts Council offered him its prize for *Epoch and Artist* (1959), a collection of prose criticism, letters, prefaces, and book reviews gathered by Jones's personal friend Harman Grisewood. In 1961 he was elected Fellow of the Royal Society of Literature, and in 1974 made Companion of Honour in the Queen's Birthday list. The 1960s and early 1970s also brought new editions of *In Parenthesis* and *The Anathemata*, special editions of *Poetry Wales* and *Agenda* magazine devoted entirely to David Jones, and the serious beginnings of interest in scholarly circles.

The poems that make up Jones's last major volume, *The Sleeping Lord*, had their first publication variously in periodicals from 1955 to 1968. A footnote to "The Wall," however, is typical: "c. 1952, but using, in part some fragments written c. 1940" (*SL*, p. 14). It is accurate to say that all Jones's poetry was always "in progress"; these verse fragments were once described by Jones as "all the pieces I left out of *The Anathemata*,"[46] and while he and his readers hoped that he would in his late years bring together these fragments into an ordered work that would be a worthy sequel to that poem, it was not to be. In theme, subject (based largely upon Arthuriana, *The Mabinogion*, the musings of Roman soldiery at the time of the Crucifixion), and verse form or style they are unmistakably the work of David Jones and hark back to his earliest writing in *In Parenthesis*. Repetitive in some respects, perhaps, but not self-imitative and literally unimitatable, the poems of *The Sleeping Lord*, published but a few months before he died, make a fitting conclusion to his life and work.

Jones moved in 1962 to a residential hotel in Harrow, named, aptly, "Monksdene," and lived and worked there until 1970, when he suffered a stroke and subsequently a broken femur. He then became a patient in the Calvary Nursing Home, also in Harrow, in the care of the Nuns of the Little Company of Mary until his death on October 28, 1974, four days short of his seventy-ninth birthday. His life in his last decade was nothing like retirement; he was busily engaged in reworking his manuscripts; creating Romanic calligraphy for personal Christmas cards, friends' book jackets and, of course, his own; affixing his signature to subscribed, limited editions of his work (*The Fatigue, The Tribune's Visitation*, a new edition with long introduction and his own engravings of *The Rime of the Ancient Mariner*); answering correspondence from near and far; receiving friends and inquiring scholars in his cluttered, confined room; writing occasional letters to the editors of *The Times* and the *Listener*; being interviewed on tape at some length. He was offered "hundreds" for his paintings, in the world in which, he said, "I sold my early paintings for nothing.' "[47] But they were not for sale.

His words to H. S. Ede in the early 1940s held to describe his outlook late in life: "I like looking out on to the world from a reasonably sheltered position. I can't paint in the wind, and I like the indoors outdoors, contained yet limitless feeling of windows and doors. A man should be in a house; a beast should be in a field, and all that."[48] While the reputation of Dylan Thomas, a fellow Anglo-Welsh poet, is and was dependent to a large, perhaps excessive extent on his public image and performance, Jones's remained shadowed:

Over the last fifteen years or so I have occasionally read such things as *The Tutelar of the Place, The Dream of Private Clitus*, and also very occasionally given "talks"; I've only once done anything on T.V.... I have *never* taken part in any conferences or congresses ... though I have sometimes been invited to do so. But the truth is that *I am quite incapable of taking part in public debates or giving lectures.* This is partly owing to ill-health and partly, I suppose, to temperament, or whatever the word is.[49]

He described himself as "little politically minded," but suggested publicly, when *The Times* contended that "political nationism in Wales is often stupid and unreal," that "such trends of opinion occurring in a people are most certainly an indication of unfulfilled needs of some sort."[50] Complaining about the reduction in Third Programme broadcasts, he deferred — "one is necessarily very much aware of not being conversant with the complex and inter-related data upon which, no doubt, the decision was based" — and then expressed opposition to that "something in the prevailing mood of our particular society" to which the BBC felt obliged to cater.[51] It was a voice gentle and assured and persuasive, without resort to stridency or invective.

He expressed few regrets, but felt one loss particularly strongly, that *yr hen iaith Gymraeg* was not handed on to him by his father. In the same tone he lamented that "there are Welsh-speaking Welshmen even today who are quite indifferent to this [language] heritage and some who think that it has no place in the world of today. Such an attitude I regard rather as I regard those in the Roman Church (to which I belong) who are indifferent to the Latin liturgy, a heritage which is theirs to conserve."[52] The last word is singularly important, not because it pegs Jones as a reactionary in the political or ideological scheme, but because it sums his essential pattern of thought, his essential ideas on the role of the artist, which he saw as being to re-present, to validate the signs of the past, to keep open the lines of communication from antiquity to the present. In that sense he is the most "conservative" or "conserva-tionist" of poets.

David Jones's reputation will rest higher in literature than it ever was in painting. It is a mark of his potential wider appreciation and importance to see that he can be included, indeed must be reckoned with, in such diverse coteries of literature as the Anglo-Welsh, the Catholic, the World War I poets, and the main-line modernists and myth-psychological poets. London-Welshman he indeed was, but in all his art David Jones defies the tag of regionalist. "The differ-ence between the present and the past," Eliot wrote, "is that the conscious present is an awareness of the past in a way and to an extent which the past's awareness of itself cannot show."[53] David Jones's major work is a "perpetual showing" of the past in the present; not of himself as subject in a fixed, locatable time, but of man, ancient and modern, at war and at worship.

CHAPTER 2

Epoch and Artist

I   *Introduction*

T HE essays, prefaces, reviews, and letters which are gathered in
Epoch and Artist are divided into four main subdivisions. Section I, including "Autobiographical Talk" and the Preface to *In
Parenthesis*, is concerned primarily with things Welsh; Section II,
perhaps the weightiest, is largely given over to an examination of
Roman Catholic theology and its relation to aesthetics and man's
place in the modern world; it includes a reprinting of the Preface to
The Anathemata; Section III deals with the Arthurian history and
legend, its treatment in the worlds of archaeology and literature
and meaning for moderns; Section IV, the shortest, includes pieces
on Eric Gill, Christopher Smart, and James Joyce, and can be seen
as exercises in applied criticism emerging from, yet distinctly different in kind than, the theory and philosophical enquiry which
precedes them and are the heart of *Epoch and Artist*. The writings
are dated variously from 1937 to 1958; some are modified considerably from their first drafts or appearance in print.

Merely to recite Jones's chief philosophical concerns in this volume — the nature of art and its connection, as sacrament, to religion; the "Matter of Britain" in Medieval Romance, its historical, archaeological, and linguistic "deposits" and their continuing
meaning in the present "civilizational situation" — is to perceive
the wide scope and high seriousness of Jones's interests. His mind
was, by his own statement, of a wool-gathering type, albeit opera-
ting at a high intellectual level (to consider a tapestry as a "wool-
gathering" helps perhaps to dignify the phrase), and his methods
can be seen as, at least initially, associationist. By the norms of
academe he was an amateur; he had no formal university educa-

tion, no bibliography of monographs in learned journals, and for this lack he expressed no regret and made no apology. He wrote to Vernon Watkins in a letter of April 29, 1953: "Well, I've no scholarship — I've just nosed about as best I can to find out the things I wanted to know or check up on things I half knew or had received fm this source or that."[1]

No "scholar" in a formal sense, perhaps, but as is evidenced clearly in this collection of prose essays he was indeed a widely read and learned man, scrupulously precise in his use of the language (or languages) and at great pains to define, usually with reference to root meanings and prior literary usage, the terms he used. The essays, true to the etymology of that word, are characterized by a spirit of enquiry; rarely can their tone be decribed as authoritarian or didactic. Jones was consciously and humbly aware always, particularly when dealing with material from medieval times and before, that there is more, far more, lost than is preserved. Nevertheless, his attitude is always that the artist must work with the "deposits" of which he has knowledge, "work within the limits of his love," and engage the difficulties caused by the accidents of history, that which we see (in a variation on St. Paul) but "darkly in a mirror." The essays include a great deal of quasi-historical and legendary hearsay, but it is always clearly identified as such. The footnotes rarely establish or assert final authority; instead they are a continuation in style and sometimes argument of the allusive, browsing methods of the main body of the essay. The deliberate craftsmanship, accomplished precision "carpentry" which Jones saw as being at the heart of all artistic endeavor, is more in evidence in the poetry, where the rigors of syllogism and documented and accountable references are not called for, where the language is intended to embody its meaning, to be a tangible "sign," and not be in the service of *Prudentia*, a means to another end.

To look but briefly here at the prefaces to *In Parenthesis* and *The Anathemata* is to point out that difference and to raise the question of why those prefaces are necessary. Jones wrote very sparingly on the visual arts, and rarely included notes of introduction to, or explanatory notes for, his paintings. Why, then, must his long poems be so accompanied? Jones answered the question at some length in the preface to *The Anathemata*, which I discuss in Chapter 4; the evident answer is that he felt that since he was writing for an audience with which he did not have a "shared background," he had to try to explain his intentions and *modus operandi* to help bring about a prior measure of understanding between reader and poet. He knew he was writing "difficult" poetry, but found the difficulty in it quite indispensable; there was just no getting around it if the poet was to be true to his "deposits" and to the complexities of his own time. At the same time, Jones felt under a heavy obligation to assist his reader.

Another answer lies, I think, in the observation that his late adoption and embrace of the written word as prime medium was near total. Whatever his achievement as a painter and engraver, his works in those media were in some vital way deficient, less than complete. With regard to his painting, Jones felt that it could stand alone, indeed that it must, even though in so standing it left something vital about itself, its intentions or meanings, unsaid. But by the late 1920s, with a firm and assured understanding of the relation of religion and art in sacrament, came a new sense of urgency, one that could not abide the possibility of less than total understanding — an urgency, finally, that demanded of the artist that he summon and use all his resources, painting, engraving, drawing, lettering, prose (in footnotes and prefaces) all in one volume; all in the service of and attendant upon the one presentation at the center, which was the poetry. The prose then in Jones is *Prudentia* serving *Ars*; *Ars* is not her handmaiden. The poems are not written in justification of their prefaces, though they might be seen to exemplify them. But there should be no mistaking the priorities.

"Art," Jones writes, "is the distinguishing dignity of man" (p. 89); it is the distinctive and justifying definition of him in Creation. All men from the beginning of time have been and are makers of artworks; man so defined performs a sacramental act involving remembrance, celebration, offering, and anticipation of the future whether he is writing an epic poem, celebrating the Communion, or baking a cake for his child's birthday. The threat Jones perceived in the age of technocracy was and is that this essentially spiritual or sacramental impulse in man will be crushed or subverted to a wholly utilitarian drive. It was a threat that, I think it is fair to say, Jones found in his own concerns; the pieces in *Epoch and Artist* "do not comprise a made work — far from it. That indeed is one of the reasons why they are not much to my liking. They were written for this or that didactic purpose and that is not really my game" (p. 17).

I deal in more detail with the prefaces to *In Parenthesis* and *The Anathemata* in the chapters devoted to those poems; here I shall look at three other essays, one each from Sections I, II, and III, respectively, but not in that order. Rather, chronologically by date of first publication, they are "The Myth of Arthur" (1941), "Wales and the Crown" (1953), and "Art and Sacrament" (1955).

II *"The Myth of Arthur"*

The essay was written first "under somewhat unsatisfactory conditions in 1940–41" and revised extensively for inclusion in *Epoch and Artist*. It is a major piece, forty-seven pages long, and displays erudition and scholarship of a uniquely imaginative variety. That is, Jones is concerned not merely to trace in chronological fashion the origins and various renditions of the story of Arthur, but more importantly to weave among those sources of "historical mythus" to see what significance the myth has had in Western history and if and how it can be seen to retain significance for moderns. He touches upon or reviews, as it were, the varied theories in scholarship as to the origins of Arthur, but his own contribution is not to quarrel with or quibble over details of "fact" or chronology or influence or literary "borrowing"; rather it is to enquire and attempt to answer just "how came this ruling-class Romano-Briton ... to be the focal point of medieval romance in Britain, France, Germany, indeed all the West?" (pp. 213–214).

The essay focuses specifically on the Welsh ingredient in the collected Arthuriana that makes up the historic "Matter of Britain," not in the cause of nationalist drum-beating but because that contribution is of abiding concern to the Welsh, whom Jones sees as having always had, despite periodic urges for separatism, a devotion to the unity of the island. Jones is concerned not to elevate Arthur in a narrow nationalistic way, but to see him in his many shapes:

Dux bellorum says the historian, Emperor of the West says the bogus relic, the king once and the king who shall be says the Christian romance writer, the mysterious chief, for whose funeral-mound it would be unwise to search, says the bardic tradition (p. 213).

Nennius, the unnamed Welsh bards, Malory, and Geoffrey of Monmouth are his prime sources; he alludes further to Chaucer, Drayton, Spenser, Milton, Blake, Tennyson, and in the twentieth century, Charles Williams, all poets who touch in some way on the figure of Arthur. This matter is our "inscape," Jones writes, and man, "whether on pre-history hill-camp, or in city-state, or in medieval manor, in the world of the primitive migrations or of imperial collapse, in Victorian security or in our own Neo-Georgian predicament ... can, must, and does make a song about it" (p. 241). He is perfectly aware that "whilst one comes across individuals for whom Malory is an essential part of their luggage, it cannot be said that the Arthur saga has any great place in the consciousness of the mass of our countrymen" (p. 215). But that is their loss to the extent that they are now knowledgeable about it; it is their gain, or at any event inescapable in that it forms the tradition of which they are inevitably a part. The Arthurian "deposits" are in total — archaeological, linguistic, historical, legendary, religious — his countrymen's whole cultural conditioning, and "all thing connected with this tangle should be of interest to people of this island, because it is an affair of our own soil and blood and tradition, our own 'inscape' "(p. 243).

The preeminent Arthurian for Jones is Malory. His *Morte Darthur* was written at just the right time in history, Jones notes; "a little later and it would have been a romantic rather than a romance document" (p. 244). Malory's preeminence for Jones lay in the way his experience, reading, and imagination were able to function together in the crafting of the language:

His data (his visual, felt data I mean), were accurate, experiential and contactual. And something of that sort is a necessity to the making of a work, there can be no getting round that necessity in the long run. The imagination must work through what is known and known by a kind of touch. Like the Yggdrasil of northern myth, the roots must be in hard material though the leaves be conceptual and in the clouds; otherwise we can have fancy but hardly imagination (p. 244).

The kind of allegorical or baroque overlay that Spenser and/or Milton (had the latter proceeded with his intended Arthuriad instead of justifying the Fall) brought to English poetry was alien to Jones. He wonders too if Tennyson would have dared proceed with his *Idylls of the King* had Milton engaged the same theme. He does not object that Tennyson "invested his subject with the values of his own age," which no poet can escape, but complains of what he left out: "the whole weight of what lies hidden — the many strata of it" (p. 234). It is that quality of missing nothing which Jones sees in Malory, the most successful, in his eyes, miner of the deposits of Arthurian myth. Jones quotes from various passages of *Morte Darthur* at some length to establish "the variation in range of Malory's gunnery" — an instance of Jones's frequent use of military metaphor: "But whether grave, gay, profane or sacred, of the contingent or the absolute, all is held within the restraint of an extremely economical, deceptively simple, native English prose style. The explosiveness of the content never cheapens the form or otherwise hurts the shape of the writing" (p. 250). In short, the work has first to be valid for its own time if it is to have present or future worth as currency. *Morte Darthur* is authentic in its contactual language, and Jones asserts that Malory's account, despite its being "very late medieval English translation from early medieval French material," is, in the most serious sense of the word, truly "creative," capturing not only the past in the present but capable of projecting itself forward in time to inform all subsequent accounts.

Arthur himself (or himselves) has become, as used by various propagandists of various persuasions for various reasons, potentially all things to all men. He is "the conveyer of order, even to the confines of chaos; he is redeemer, in the strict sense of the word; he darkens the Lombard threshold only with his weapon; his potency is the instrument of redemption. . . . Always the consolidater, the saviour and the channel of power, the protector and gift-giver, and more significantly for us, 'The Director of Toil' " (p. 237). To some extent this essay, indeed, all of Section III of *Epoch and Artist*, might well be read as a preface to Jones's own Arthurian poems, "The Sleeping Lord" and "The Hunt," the latter dealing with Arthur's leadership of the hunt of the great Boar Trwyth as first told in *"Culhwch ac Olwen"* in the *Mabinogion*. In both poems Arthur is elaborated far beyond the warring Romano-Briton to be identified with Christ, as is evident in the passage quoted in words like "redeemer" and "saviour," but Jones's initial concern with Arthur is in the Welsh context.

"We know," he writes, "that in ninth-century Wales Arthur was already a marvel-figure . . . already quasi-mythological" (p. 225). But then something happened: Geoffrey of Monmouth's *Historia Regum Brittaniae* (1137) was translated from Latin into Welsh and French and its "contrived and composite story with its contemporary twelfth-century slant and style soon overlaid or got mixed up with the genuine native material and this cannot be regarded as other than a nuisance" (pp. 225–226). No more than a "nuisance," because it can be seen by Jones as yet another historical accident that Wales was changing inevitably anyway. But it was a loss nonetheless that the authentic part of the Welsh "historical mythus" suffered "romancing" of a sort akin to the English "literary convention mixed with locality-traditions as at Glastonbury and else-where'' (p. 227). Still, Jones insists, no English poet of the thir-teenth century, ''without affectation, artificiality, or loss of that necessary liaison with the concrete (without which all art falters)'' could have referred, as did the bard of Llywelyn in lamenting that Welsh prince killed in 1282, to the death of Arthur, as in the line (translated from the Welsh): ''Much the piteous crying, as at Cam-lann, much the weeping'' (p. 227). It remained for Malory to weld together the various figures of Arthur, whose presence was by that time, Jones asserts, ''part of the shared inheritance of Welshmen and Englishmen,'' into the definitive, shaped, authentic work: in short, to validate the ''deposits.'' That an Englishman from War-wickshire produced the authentic goods when the Welshman Geoffrey produced only mischief is to be perceived as another of those fortuitous accidents that adds to the ''*complexity* of our tra-dition'' and to the historical unity of the island: ''We must not have too great a passion for continuous definition'' (p. 237).

The Arthurian material is not for Jones of mere academic inter-est; it is one of his most important background sources and referents. But beyond even that it is central to his whole vision of man in twentieth-century civilization. All the ''deposits'' whether of mythology, history, or romance tell us that ''God is wonderful,'' Jones writes, but they tell us also that when the ''realm is 'wholly mischiefed' '' there is no clear sign of that which will restore it or allow the wonder of God to show itself. Jones proposes that in the figure of Arthur-Christ, ''from the machine age the strayed machine-men may create a myth patient of baptism'' (p. 259). It is at least his hope. He does not consciously promote himself as a modern Malory or as the poet best qualified by ancestry or history to revitalize Arthur for his time, but the qualities he perceived in Malory are the standards he set for himself, as a thorough reading of the prefaces and indeed the poems themselves will verify:

To conserve, to develop, to bring together, to make significant for the present what the past holds, without dilution or any deleting, but rather by understanding and transubstantiating the material, this is the function of genuine myth, neither pedantic nor popularizing, not indifferent to schol-arship, nor antiquarian, but saying always: ''of these thou hast given me have I lost none'' (p. 243).

III   *"Wales and the Crown"*

''Wales and the Crown'' is an occasional piece, first written for broadcast on the Welsh Home Service of the BBC on July 23, 1953, in celebration of the coronation of Queen Elizabeth II. It follows from, in many respects, his "Myth of Arthur" essay, in that Jones is at great pains to demonstrate the unique Welsh contribution to the unity of the British island not only in historic persons and events, but more subtly and importantly, via the Arthurian material, and more speculatively but most importantly, in the Celtic matriarchal influence which he sees as reemerging in the accession of the young queen.

The Welshness of all this represents still only a part of the essay, which enlarges on Jones's ideas of sacrament and "anathemata" (his poem by that title was published in the preceding year). That those ideas are introduced into the "Wales and the Crown" context at all is worth noting; but they clearly belong and are not forced.

Jones, as Eliot declared himself to be, was a "Royalist" in politics, though he must have had conflicts and doubts later. (It is of pertinent interest that he became a close friend of Saunders Lewis, a Welsh poet, dramatist, political thinker and activist, and another Catholic convert, but radically different from Jones in that he was the founder of *Plaid Cymru*, the Welsh Nationalist party, whose ultimate aim is to free Wales of subjection to Westminster. The two men retained the highest affection and respect for each other. Another close friend of Jones's was Valerie Gwynne-Williams, who ran as the *Blaid's* candidate for a parliamentary seat.) There was certainly a change in the political climate of Wales in the years from Elizabeth's coronation to her investiture of Charles as Prince of Wales in 1969, but Jones never was either outspokenly nor by implication a "separatist," though he applauded Saunders Lewis as "a man of particular *pietas* toward his Welsh heritage and who is known for his passionate but reasoned love toward and defence of the language."[2] One suspects that for Jones, further research and archaeological digging into "the excavation at Sycharth, the main residence of Owain Glyn Dŵr"[3] is more to be commended than overt political action, particularly of the sort for which Saunders Lewis was once jailed. Jones notes too that Glyn Dŵr had proposed two universities, or *studia generalia*, for Wales as early as the fourteenth century before disappearing as an outlaw or guerrilla and passing into the folklore of Wales; Jones celebrates him for his learning, his ideas. A critic once suggested that "perhaps David Jones is only able to sustain his illusion . . . because he himself lives near London and takes care not to confront himself too sharply with the realities of life as it is lived in Wales."[4] But for Jones the

so-called "realities" had roots deeper by far than political commentary of the time could ever understand.

Jones's view of history as largely "accidental" does not require
that it be seen as merely haphazard, an amalgam of unrelated
events. Wales "emerged as it was *per accidens* and as a survival
from the disintegration of what had been the Diocese of Britain."
In that sense its history predates and is different from that of the
Angles, Picts, Saxons, and Scots which were "forces exterior to
and ... invaders of the disintegrating provinces of the Empire"
(p. 45). That is, the Romanized Celts pre-occupied the land, and
while one view of history might hold them to have been defeated, in
Jones's view that is a mere tampering with the outward formalities,
as it were; the conquerors are themselves caught up in, modified
by, and subject to the more ancient order and mythologies. It is
"axiomatic that the origin of things conditions their ends in
however obscure, roundabout, mutated or even quite contradictory
a manner" (p. 45). To invoke a codified or sequential "system"; to
retail the *dicta* of Kings and Acts of Parliament as the determiners
of history, is to misread the past and mislead oneself. Jones is happiest in the world of complexity, mystery: "A great confluity and
dapple, things counter, pied, fragmented, twisted, lost: that is
indeed the shape of things all over Britain, but Wales has her own
double-dapple" (p. 46). This is language right out of Hopkins, and
there is no dictionary that can define "double-dapple" to an un-
trusting or unbelieving skeptic. Jones goes on with another word
from Hopkins, haeccity, or "this-ness"; these are things unique
in the historical and cultural past — tangled skeins, buried "deposits," the testimony of centuries of neglect, conflict, forgetfulness,
deceit, glory. The Welsh "things set up, lifted up, or in whatever
manner made over to the gods" (to borrow from his definition of
"anathemata" (*A*, p. 29) make up the Welsh offering on this
coronation day. It is "an assortment of gifts in one, small, home-
made basket" (p. 47), and that basket contains all that is Wales in
legend, history, quasi-history, and prehistory. Not given grudgingly
by the conquered to the conqueror, it includes a particular blessing
from and upon matriarchy, the blessing of Helena, "the eternal
matriarch," who, Jones asserts, "passes from pseudohistory into
the realm of true myth" and through Elizabeth II into the second
half of the twentieth century.

It is an ingenious argument cleverly and seriously made, but not
likely to calm the passions of Welsh dissidents or poor hill-farmers,

underpaid coal miners, or the unemployed. But "anathemata" cannot be, by Jones's definitions, abstractions such as virtue, love, or loyalty. Anathemata are always the visible and concrete signs, or *signa*. It is these which, when offered to the proper recipient, be she Queen of England or the Virgin Mary, take on sacramental quality. Yet Jones does not denote precisely what visible, tangible "things" are in the Welsh basket. It cannot be denied that there is that uniquely Welsh contribution to the British crown and monarchy that consists of the mixture of history and legend. But to hold that these gifts are, by Jones's own definition, "sacramental" is another problem. The story he relates of Llywelyn's death, that "it was fitting that a relic of the Cross should have been found, if it was, upon his body" (p. 47), is tenuous to an extreme. Most commentators would overlook that "deposit" to dwell on the ignominy of Llywelyn's head being severed and taken to London as a prize of war. That is not the emphasis Jones wants, as his essay falls back, quite uncharacteristically, to something near exhortation: "It seems to me salutary that persons of Welsh affinity should recall this terminal event of seven centuries ago when they turn, with the rest of the people of this Island, to consider the figure, who, this summer, by specific acts and things done to her has herself been made the visible sign of that invisible thing, the concept, the Monarchy of Britain" (p. 40).

The British monarchy is for Jones a holy thing, not because it is all-wise and pure, not because of a "divine right of kings" legalistic fiat, but because it has the blessing of all British history, because the sovereign is one "set apart and made other" by the bestowal of rites and signs that are culturally and ecclesiastically valid. To one Father Crehan, who questioned in a public letter Jones's use of "sacramental" to describe the rites of coronation, Jones answered: "The impression of regal splendour, let alone of mere pomp, was altogether eclipsed by something far deeper, more primal and quite ageless. The impression was of something sacrificial. A person appeared to have been 'made *sacra*' " (p. 50). The answer is itself subject to further questioning in that words like "impression" and "appeared to" compromise the idea of tangible, concrete, visible, and unmistakable *signa*.

It may be that power resides in the office of Prime Minister, but majesty remains in the person of the Queen. And for Jones the Welsh investment in the British monarchy is deep and irreplaceable, and it is essential that it be preserved not only for Britain's but

for Wales's sake. The Welshness of the British monarchy predates
the House of Tudor; it predates even Arthur. It persists in the
island's deepest and most complex deposits, and influences the
nation in its newest day. Jones concludes on a theme that permeates
all his writings: "For remember there is the tradition of matriarchy,
a thing of pre-Celtic provenance working up through the Aryan
patriarchy. And in Wales, Y Mamau, the mothers, have always
been influential, whether as mortal women or as fairies reflecting
the cult of the Deae Matres of antiquity. . . . For we have re-entered
a matriarchal situation — perhaps in deeper ways than we as yet
understand" (p. 48).

IV   *"Art and Sacrament"*

In some respects the most important, and certainly the most
complete examination of the relation between his aesthetics and
religious philosophy, this essay is at the same time the least characteristic, least pleasing, of Jones's prose works. Its earnestness and
seriousness are not to be denied, however, and Jones has recourse
to two basic strategies to put across his thesis: argument by the syllogism of abstractions (quite uncharacteristic), and argument by
analogy and metaphor. With the second method Jones is happier; it
is the method of the poet, seeking the concrete, the tangible, in the
tangle of theological and philosophical abstraction. The essay's
subtitle, "An Enquiry Concerning the Arts of Man and the Christian Commitment to Sacrament in Relation to Contemporary Technocracy," reads like the prospectus for an academic thesis, but the
word "enquiry" is important; it is the equivalent for his prose of
"fragments" or "attempted writing," words which Jones used to
describe his poetry. Frequently in the essay Jones remarks, in diffident asides, that his work is only an enquiry, a venture into
troubled waters, and that the reader should not expect too much,
maybe a "fortunate landfall or two." Jones seems often to be
unsatisfied with his own remarks and progress, and even felt
obliged to append a supplementary short essay to explain further
his definition of "utile," a key word in the main essay. There is evidence throughout that Jones, while perhaps welcoming the opportunity to expound at length on so important a theme, was himself
dissatisfied with the academic and metaphysical tone of his accomplishment.

"Art and Sacrament" was written in 1955 for a collection of
essays by prominent Catholic thinkers in which they were invited to
discuss, from the common ground of their subscription to Catho-

licism, what each saw as the unique dilemma of his chosen vocation or avocation. Jones, as representative of the "arts," immediately removes his contribution from the realm of "propositions of faith and propositions of morals" to insist that "there are then no such things as the Catholic arts of painting and engraving or the Catholic art of writing proses or poems" (p. 144). Just as, he notes for comparison, there is no such thing as the Calvinistic-Methodist art of boxing. Still, Jones writes as a Catholic artist, and "certain charts of Catholic and pre-Catholic provenance will be found relevant to our task." It is not the Church as agent of redemption or spokesman for God, and certainly not the Church as guardian of public morals or ethics that holds him; rather it is the Church as guardian of the holiest art forms, which she preserves and daily validates and witnesses to in the enactment of the sacraments, that of the Eucharist in particular.

In Jones's theology, God is the ultimate artist; His creation of the universe was an act, not necessarily of divine beneficence and certainly not of divine necessity, but most assuredly of divine gratuitousness, having no taint of the utilitarian except *post facto*. Man, a creature made in the image of his Maker, is the unique functioning artist on earth. It is to man alone, and not to the lower animals or to the angels, that the gift of the capacity for gratuitous "making" is privileged. Man alone among God's creatures "creates," by which Jones means always gathers together, remembers, recalls, shapes, molds, forms, makes objects whose end is delight, which is the only necessary end of art. Man is also a creature of utility, a "prudential animal," but in all his works there attaches a secondary quality of "gratuitousness" that goes beyond the barest functionalism.

Jones proposes that the nature of art and of man as an art-making creature is evidenced in all man's works: "things as dissimilar as: the Diesel engine, boot-making, English prose, radar, horticulture, carpentry and the celebration of the Sacred Mysteries" (p. 153). He goes on to isolate, for example, four specific categories of "making": strategy, the preparing of "Susan's birthday cake," celebration of the Eucharist, and Hogarth's painting *The Shrimp Girl*. He chooses "strategy" since the word is free of typical "artistic" associations and would seem to be concerned with getting things done rather than the "making" of a thing. For Jones, however, strategy does partake of art in that "man-as-strategist is concerned with a positioning, and so a juxtaposing, of cer-

tain several parts with a view to establishing a certain whole ... by
which activity a form, not previously existent, is created." Insofar
then as it partakes of art, it partakes necessarily of *religio*,
that "which binds man to God" (p. 159). Thus man's newest
"strategy" is that which links him inevitably to the "archetypal
form-making" that was God's in the creation of the world. That
was a sign of God's gratuitous nature; and man the creator also is
inextricably a "sign-maker." Christ's intercession on the cross was
a further sign of his gratuitous nature, and it is celebrated in the
"sign" or strategic artwork he commanded for his remembrance in
the Sacrament of the Eucharist. Man's reenactment of that sign recalls and revalidates it and himself as man and signmaking creature. When man celebrates by preparing his child's birthday cake,
this action too is "pre-ordained to Ars, from the first movement of
the cook's mind to make something that should be significant of
Susan's birth"; this too by definition partakes of *religio*.

But certainly all the conditions, determining what is art from what is not,
are more than fulfilled. There is making, there is added making, there is
explicit sign, there is a showing forth, a re-presenting, a recalling and there
is gratuitousness and there is full intention to make this making thus.
Moreover this particular making signifies a birth. It recalls a past event
and looks back at some anniversaries and looks forward to future anniversaries; it is essentially celebrative and festal: it would be gay. For as
Poussin said of another art: "The goal of painting is delight." And this is
universally true of all art no matter how difficult it is to posit the delight
(p. 164).

In short, this seemingly trivial event has in it the same elements as
make up the sacrament of celebrating the Last Supper. For Jones,
the most significant words Christ ever uttered were those in which
He took the bread and wine and said, "Do this ... in remembrance
of me." "Now the crucial question is," Jones write, "why did the
Lord employ artforms and establish a tradition commanding the
continued employment of those forms?" (p. 162). And to look
finally at the example of a "classic" painting; to say that it is representative or realistic is to avoid saying "what that work in fact *is*."
To hyphenate "re-presentative," and Jones customarily does,
makes Jones's intention a little more clear. But still, what may it be
said to "represent"? The origin of the painting, whether done from
a model or an actual fish-girl, is irrelevant; what Hogarth had in
mind or intended to do so is irrelevant; the painting is its own thing,
"an object contrived various materials and so ordered by

Hogarth's muse as to show forth, recall and re-present, strictly within the conditions of a given art and under another mode, such and such a reality. It is a *signum* of that reality and it makes a kind of anamnesis of that reality'' (p. 174).

As Jones defines him, it is in his art that man asserts, celebrates, and validates his manhood; in the Roman Catholic Church and its "art-forms" he participates in his godhood. It was from such perceptions that Jones became a Catholic convert, though he was to deplore the demythologizing, deritualizing of the Church, and to deplore the passing of the Latin liturgy of the Tridentine Mass particularly. It is accurate to say, however, that within this subscription Jones is finally an advocate of "art for art's sake." He is not a follower of the decadents, but does not disavow entirely the validity of that "somewhat wild, dated and naughty saying" except as it invites misunderstanding (p. 149). He prefers: "Art is the sole intransitive activity of man," and the high Latinate language that asserts the primacy of *Ars* over *Prudentia*. Art is neither the servant of moral persuasion nor its medium, and this is why there can be no Catholic art — or Capitalist art, Welsh art, Marxist art, etc. "While *Prudentia* is exercised about our intentions, *Ars* is concerned with the shape of a finished article," Jones wrote in the preface to *The Anathemata*, and he bypasses completely critical arguments to artistic intention or effect. Man's way to self-definition is as an artist; he is "unavoidably a sacramentalist and . . . his works are sacramental in character" (p. 155). Also absent is any notion of moral imperative or submission to authority; art is man fulfilling, literally, himself, which is quite other than mere selfishness or self-indulgence. Man does not celebrate the Mass because of the threat of excommunication in this life and outer darkness in the next, Jones implies; he celebrates it as an art-making creature. "But," Jones adds, "even if we are Christians holding a belief at the furthest possible remove from this Catholic belief we are still committed to the notion of sign." Still further, one does not have to be Christian at all: "we are committed to sign in virtue of being men" (p. 168).

It is then finally the most catholic of world-views that Jones avers. To trace unmistakably the logic of the argument from capitalized to lowercase "catholic": at the Last Supper, on what we now call Maundy Thursday, it was rite-making and sign-making by and on behalf of God made flesh which made valid and visible in art forms "what was done on the Hill." The Christian faith is not a matter of moral behavior nor is it a matter for, in a Platonic sense, an idealist view of man. It does not consist in denial of the body or assert the primacy of spirit over the corporeal. In the doctrine of transubstantiation it is the physical presence of the "made-over" corporeal body of Christ that is celebrated. And man, in his physical presence, alone can celebrate the rite of the Eucharist; man alone can make anathemata as he handles the objects made *sacra*: "Angels can't, nor can the beasts.... Without body: without sacrament. Angels only: no sacrament. Beasts only: no sacrament. Man: sacrament at every turn and all levels of the 'profane' and 'sacred,' in the trivial and in the profound, no escape from sacrament" (p. 167).

V *Conclusion*

Jones can be described as neither literary critic nor historian, though the prose writing in *Epoch and Artist* include a great deal of history, political and literary, and he does occasionally make judgments of the writings of other artists. He was not a social critic, nor was he a professional theologian or philosopher of aesthetics. He was a practicing artist, a practicing Roman Catholic; and while he enlisted the language of one subscription in support of the other and applied the language of both to the outer world, the war, specifically, and his "civilizational situation" in the world of technocracy, he did not invoke them on behalf of capitalized High Culture or political morality or action. He was both Welsh and British without being intense and chauvinist. Art for him is not to be seen as a trickle-down system; it is the one great equalizer, the one possession common to all men, the sole valid mediator between God and man. To quote him in his accustomed military terminology: "Ars is adamant about one thing: she compels you to do an infantryman's job. She insists on the tactile. The artist in man is the infantryman in man.... All men are aboriginally *of* this infantry" (p. 183).

"Art and Sacrament" ends with Jones's citing a verse fragment he had abandoned in 1938 (it was later rewritten and titled "*A, a, a Domine Deus*") which is a personal statement of the "dilemmas and quandaries" that beset him and underlie the concerns and thesis of that essay. The fragment concludes: "For it is easy to miss him at the turn of a civilization," in which the "him" is not capitalized, and significantly not so; for while the poem is a brief account of a frustrated search for God, it can be read throughout as a recounting of Jones's search for man-the-artist in the modern age.

CHAPTER 3

In Parenthesis

I *Introduction*

I used to stay in a house at Portslade, near Brighton.... In 1928, at this bungalow...I began to write down some sentences which turned out to be the initial passages of *In Parenthesis*, published some ten years later.

This was a beginning of another sort. I had no idea of what I was letting myself in for.[1]

The casual reader having just completed *In Parenthesis* might well echo that last sentiment. If he had thought to read briskly just another "war novel" or trench autobiography, he has been quickly disabused, and his first instinct might well be to try to pin a descriptive label on the book before him. Other decidedly noncasual readers have had the same impulse, but the book resists easy categorizing. T. S. Eliot, who read the manuscript at Faber in typescript, was not to be drawn into having to label it "prose" or "poetry" ("with the implication that it is neither"), and was able throughout his note of introduction to a 1961 reprinting to refer to it merely as a "book"; later he was to concede, if grudgingly, that it could be regarded as a "war book," if indeed the question mattered at all. Most critics, however, have followed the lead of Herbert Read, who called it "as near a great epic of the war as the war generation will reach,"[2] and Stephen Spender, for whom it was the "monumental elegy of World War I," for too long neglected, he wrote, because "it is not clear to its critics, nor to its author's fellow poets, that it is poetry."[3] David Jones, however, had his own word for his creation; it is a "writing," and it is a word he insists upon in the preface to *In Parenthesis*.

II *The Preface*

"This writing has to do with some things I saw, felt, & was part of" (*IP*, p. ix). He uses the word as a substantive seven times in the preface and once again in the dedication; further, he does not refer to the book as something *written*, rather as something that is *made*. "A day came. . . when I found myself trying my hand at the making of a writing." It was to be a nine-year undertaking for the artist, heretofore, in wood, copper, and watercolors. He elaborated further on his intentions and of the book's genesis in an interview:

> It was a thing, you know, when I wanted simply to see how you would shape an experience in words. I know the difference in drawing a line that is merely reality and getting it right so that it is a part of a composition, but I did not know then the way you would make a form out of words. I get so cross with people who say, "David Jones has preciously said he wanted to make a form in words." There is nothing precious in it.[4]

Jones notes in his preface "a consciousness of the past, the very remote, and the more immediate and trivial past, both superficially and more subtly" that was his in the actual experience of the trenches and, by extension, "during the making of this writing." Mere reportorial "reality" is not enough; self-consciousness is not enough; consciousness of the past is not enough; there must be a shaping, an ordering, a "re-presenting": "I have only tried to make a shape in words, using as data the complex of sights, sounds, fears, hopes, apprehensions, smells, things exterior and interior, the landscape and paraphernalia of that singular time and of those particular men" (p. x). The "making" denies the principle of a self-evolving organicism; it denies "free" expression; it demands the collecting, forming, shaping, constructing, the sculpturing, almost, of a tangible object.

"I have tried," Jones continues in the preface, "to so make this writing for anyone who would care to play Welsh Queen," identifying himself and his intentions with the demands made upon the Bard of the Household, according to the Welsh Codes, who sings his Queen to slumber: "He is instructed to sing first to her a song in honour of God. He must then sing the song of the Battle of Camlann — the song of treachery and of the undoing of all things; and afterward he must sing any song she may choose to hear" (p. xiii). His self-identification with the ancient Bard of the Household is stated and deliberate, and is not to be dismissed as either quaint or presumptuous. He was to write later of the bardic role and its relation to his conception of himself in the role of "maker": "As Sir Ifor Williams tells us, the bards of an earlier Wales referred to themselves as 'carpenters of song'. Carpentry suggests a fitting together and as you know the English word 'artist' means, at root, someone concerned with a fitting of some sort" (*E&A*, p. 29).

It is the "present moment of the past," in Eliot's words, not the past as history, which is the artist's in some way to establish. Jones notes with wry sadness that it is ours somehow to find ways to ennoble our new media of destruction (including "trench-mortars," "new-fangled technicalities," "exacting mechanical devices") as we have "already ennobled and made significant our old — candle-light, fire-light, Cups, Wands and Swords, to choose at random" (p. xiv). Jones is right, of course, in recognizing "these creatures of chemicals as true extensions of ourselves"; it would seem, however, to be something else entirely to hope to "ennoble" them. "It is not easy," he writes, "in considering a trench-mortar barrage to give praise for the action proper to chemicals — full though it may be of beauty" (p. xiv). No, it is not easy, as the shell-burst at the end of Part 2 will demonstrate so tellingly. The officer who wears a sword to dress parade today can only hope, a little desperately, that it somehow enhances his person and presence; he can give precious little in return. And it is doubtful indeed that future generations will give to atomic devices, germ warheads, napalm, etc., new-found, "ennobling" virtues. Jones does well to concede, and not to belabor further, the dilemma which denies to modern authors that the "embrace of battle...[be] one with the embrace of lovers." Rightly, he says: "We doubt the decency of our own inventions, and are certainly in terror of their possibilities" (p. xiv).

"The lives of all of us [Joyce, Pound, and himself specifically]," Eliot wrote in his note of introduction, "were altered by that War, but David Jones is the only one to have fought in it." David Jones was therefore the only one of the four able to write of the experience at firsthand; and *In Parenthesis* is clearly a product of one who had at the disposal of a mature artistic intelligence the "historical sense" and the experience itself and the present insight into that experience. The preface serves, finally, only incidentally to introduce *In Parenthesis*; in the larger sense it was, in 1937, an introduction to Jones the thinker and Jones the word artist, to the ways of a man to whom the words of the language were, at that beginning in 1928, "new-fangled technicalities" with which he had to come to account and learn to shape.

It is a little shy-making for a modern critic to talk about Jones
"making" his "writings," however, and I shall call *In Parenthesis*
a poem. Before outlining its action and themes in some detail, it is
worthwhile to attempt to define a little more closely its shape, texture, and form.

III   In Parenthesis

In one sense, *In Parenthesis* is an autobiographical poem. To
quote again from the preface: "This writing has to do with some
things I saw, felt and was part of. The period covered begins early
in December 1915 and ends early in July 1916" (p. ix). But it is not
autobiography, nor even history: "None of the characters in this
writing are real persons, nor is any sequence of events historically
accurate" (p. ix). It both is and is not a war poem: "I did not in-
tend this as a 'War Book' — it happens to be concerned with war. I
should prefer it to be about a good kind of peace — but as Mandeville says, 'Of Paradys ne can I not speken propurly I was not
there' " (pp. xii–xiii). It details the actions of selected men in a battalion of the Royal Welsh Fusiliers, but there are as many Cockney
as Welsh soldiers, and while the distinctions between friend and enemy might be inescapable at the front, they are deliberately blurred
in the poem — witness the dedication:

> THIS WRITING IS FOR MY FRIENDS
> IN MIND OF ALL COMMON & HIDDEN
> MEN AND OF THE SECRET PRINCES
> AND TO THE MEMORY OF THOSE
> WITH ME IN THE COVERT . . .
> AND TO THE BEARDED INFANTRY
> WHO EXCHANGED THEIR LONG
> LOAVES WITH US AT A SECTOR'S
> BARRIER AND TO THE ENEMY
> FRONT FIGHTERS WHO SHARED OUR
> PAINS AGAINST WHOM WE FOUND
> OURSELVES BY MISADVENTURE

The work purports to deal with World War I, but Roman soldiers
at the outposts of Empire and Welsh fighting men of Aneirin's sev-
enth-century *Y Gododdin*, set in Scotland, are very real presences,
coexistent, as it were, with these Taffies and Tommies in the
trenches in 1916.

In many places *In Parenthesis* reads like a traditional prose novel. That is, characters act and react in normal, realistic ways; they speak and are spoken to, command and obey; think of past, present, or future; muse, daydream, have the requisite bodies, souls, and spirits. Time passes apace as directed by the author; conventions of grammar and syntax prevail; and the controlling hand of an omniscient narrator is firmly in evidence:

Private Watcyn calls Lance-Corporal Lewis from round an earth wall's turn, who nudges Private Ball who drags forward saturated limbs; water pours from is left boot and he lifts it clear (p. 47).

There is, however, another style much in evidence: rapid-fire, idiomatic, unidentified by speaker, a confusion of voices all clamoring for attention. This, too, is a kind of "realism" which shows itself to good advantage in dramatic readings of the poem.

Who's kidding — and shorts as well — you ask Sid Whiting at the gumboot store, straight from the 'major he said — tomorrow we go in again — no — on the left, "B's" in the craters you bet, it's "A's" turn by rights — it's the Minnies what gets you down — yes, Ducks Bill, same as where old Snell went sick from — they say the swinger's posted to another mob — we shall lament his going from us, and miss his angel voice an all and show our legs to another (p. 103).

And again there is a highly allusive, esoteric, and "scholastic" poetry, far removed (by the test of realism) from the idiom of private soldiers' speech in the trenches but carrying a special burden of mythic reference and meaning for David Jones and demanding close attention to the text and notes, and reference hunting, in both memory and nearest library, for most readers:

> She's the girl with the sparkling eyes,
> she's the Bracelet Giver,
> she's a regular draw with the labour companies,
> whereby
> the paved army-paths are hers that grid the island
>   which is her dower.
> Elen Lluyddawc she is — more she is than
> Helen Argive.
>   My mob digged the outer vallum,
> we furnished picquets;
> we staked trip-wire as a precaution at
> Troy Novaunt.

> I saw the blessèd head set under
> that kept the narrow sea inviolate
>
> (p. 81).

Other sources, not from antiquity but from snatches of nursery rhymes and music-hall songs, are not perhaps so "high-brow" but demand still a wide range of background acquaintance or sympathetic willingness to learn. Jones provided thirty-five pages of footnotes to accompany the text of his poem; much grumbled about by some, and not entirely to Jones's liking, they are thoroughly useful and indeed indispensable. They direct the reader to sources in (I list only the most important) Aneirin, Malory, Chaucer, Shakespeare, Dunbar, Coleridge, Browning, Tennyson, Lewis Carroll, Bunyan, Borrow, Kipling, Hopkins, the Bible, the *Mabinogion*, the Missal; and they provide further instruction in the terminology of weapons of war and strategies of the trenches. In short, the notes serve as background reference and for elucidation both of the mythic and historical past and of the present. Jones provides no note touching on the action and characters of the present tense of his poem, however; all of that is contained within the carefully "made" work that is the poem itself and would not suffer paraphrase or elucidation in the notes.

In Parenthesis is a poem in seven parts, or sections, and in some senses can be described in familiar, conventional terms. That is, it has purposeful movement in time and action, recognizable human characters and landscape, and a definable subject of man at war. It is arranged broadly in a linear, chronological sequence, and details the movement of a group of men in arms of all ranks from the staging grounds in England (Part 1) to their destiny seven months later in the trenches at the Somme (Part 7). But that is to simplify too much, for Jones uses, and uses with careful artistry, all the devices available to the modern poet and novelist: flashback and a-head, the "free association" of stream-of-consciousness writing, shifting point of view, abrupt juxtaposition and interpolations of speech, image, character, and scenes, which is to say nothing of his allusions to centuries distant persons and events and use of words and phrases from Latin, Welsh, French, and German.

Private 25201 Ball standing in, as it were, for Private David Jones in memory, is the central figure, but "protagonist" is too strong a word to describe his role, and he is certainly not a "hero" in any traditional sense of the word. There are other characters nearly as important as Ball, notably Lieutenant Jenkins and Lance-Corporal Aneirin Merddyn Lewis. The point, and it is an important distinction, must be made that the relative "importance" of the characters lies not in their perceived relationships and dealings with each other but in the attention David Jones pays to them, the use he makes of them, as voices or recording sensibilities. They are made to bear a heavy load of referential mythic weight, and the problem Jones has posed for himself is to see that their immediate, recognizable humanity is not diminished or obscured by their other, more "poetic" uses. *In Parenthesis* bears no resemblance to a "fox-hole" novel in which characters learn to live, love, hate, fight, and perhaps die together and in which the reader is given characteristic or stereotypical "specimens"—perhaps a requisite Jew, black, college boy, garage mechanic—and told by flashback something of each's home background—father, girl friend, wife—and hardships, triumphs, ambitions, or the like. "Archetypal" serves better to describe Jones's semifictional creations; the racial or mythic ancestry that Jones provides for them places them in the whole history of recorded time; they share the human psyche of the soldiers at Catraeth, at the Crucifixion, at Malplaquet, at Harfleur, wherever man has organized war against his own kind.

In Parenthesis is a poetic enactment of tradition and the individual in war in which today's action modifies our concepts and understanding of history and its wars, in which the actions and thoughts of David Jones's Private Ball modify our understanding of all the Privates Ball of the past, even as they of the recoverable past exert an inexorable influence on behavior today. David Jones is not a reporter, an admiring spectator, not a public-relations man for pacifism or for militarism. In chronicling the action of which he was a part, he does not seek to be an epic poet singing hymns of battle in which new heroes reenact the earth-shaking deeds of their ancestors. Without apology or special pleading, he details from intimate firsthand acquaintance with the present — and from affectionate intimacy with historical man — the minds and actions of those compelled, for whatever reason, whatever "accidents" of history and geography, to go "once more into the breach." *In Parenthesis* is not a poem either to provoke or to end a war (the poet, wrote W. B. Yeats in "On Being Asked for a War Poem," has "no gift to set a statesman right") except as it adds to the accumulation of testimony to the stupidities and brutality of history that each age must learn from or, more likely, ignore. Jones brings *In Parenthe-*

sis by its end to a magnificent climax, when the violence that has
been hovering just over the ridge throughout manifests itself and
makes unbearably clear the idiocy of trench and wood warfare. To
label Jones as pacifist is, however, no more correct than to say he is
a jingoist; he is an artist. He "makes writings," he tries to make "a
shape in words," tries to "shape the experience of the war." To
that end he gathers all the experience of the present, all the "deposits" literary, historical, mythological — not all Welsh, not all heroic
— of the past, that are available to his enquiring artistic intelligence. This includes his own experience, his own emotional bias,
his ancestral bias, his reading of the experiences and emotional bi-
ases of the men, whether friend or appointed foe, who shared the
war with him. Beyond his making of a piece of written art, Jones
asserts, rather sings, the sacramental unity of man, a gesture which
embraces far more than statements on behalf of heroism or
revulsion.

IV *Part 1*

Part 1 is titled "The Many Men So Beautiful," a line from Coleridge's *The Rime of the Ancient Mariner*. It is followed in that
poem by "And they all dead did lie: / And a thousand thousand
slimy things / Lived on; and so did I." Jones does not exploit in
any extended way the larger themes of Coleridge's poem, and there
is no discernible relationship between any of the narrative voices of
In Parenthesis and the wraith-driven Mariner. It is true, however,
that of the men introduced in Part 1 many will indeed lie dead at
the poem's end, and that "the geste . . . and the man who was on
the field . . . and who wrote the book" lived on to tell this tale.

Death in the trenches and dark woods at the Battle of the Somme
is no respecter of persons or rank or of the military hierarchy which
is carefully, if seemingly casually, established in this opening part.
In order of military rank, we are introduced to Major Lillywhite
(later characterized as "that shit"); Captain Gwynn; Lieutenant
Piers Dorian Isambard Jenkins (all of twenty years old at the outset, though he is to celebrate the coming of his maturity shortly before his death); Sergeant Snell; Corporal (later promoted to Sergeant) Quilter; Lance-Corporal Aneirin Merddyn Lewis; and Private John Ball. The hierarchy, the chain of command, established
and blessed in a long tradition, functions at first in its practiced,
orderly way, in "the coming on parade of John Ball."

He settles between numbers 4 and 5 of the rear rank. It is as ineffectual as the ostrich in her sand. Captain Gwynn does not turn or move or give any sign.

Have that man's name taken if you please, Mr. Jenkins.

Take that man's name, Sergeant Snell.

Take his name, corporal   (p. 1).

There is, however, another parallel institution, coexistent, and ultimately of a higher order, that is introduced in Part 1, and it is one which, by repeated reference throughout the poem, is to become unmistakable, all-pervasive. This is the liturgical or religious order of things, and is to be discerned first in the identification of "the silence peculiar to parade grounds and refectories" and in such language as "the liturgy of a regiment departing." Lance-Corporal Lewis is described as having "somewhere in his Welsh depths a remembrance of the nature of man, of how a lance-corporal's stripe is but held vicariously and from on high, is of one texture with an eternal economy. He brings in a manner, baptism, and metaphysical order to the bankruptcy of the occasion" (pp. 1–2). In Part 4 he will be implored by the collective voice of his communicants (in the distribution of rations and tobacco) to

> Dispense salvation,
> Strictly apportion it,
> let us taste and see,
> let us be renewed,
> for christ's sake let us be warm.
> O have a care — don't spill the precious
> O don't jog his hand — ministering   (p. 73).

And in Part 7, when the Queen of the Woods honors *post mortem* the "July noblesse," she will save special attention and have special words for "Aneirin-in-the-nullah" — but quietly, because "she was careful for the Disciplines of the Wars" (p. 186). That is, she and David Jones reserve their special honors for a mythic-liturgical order; they are not to be distributed by rank or in return for deeds in battle. Lewis the ministering priest is of greater importance than Father Martin Larkin or the chaplains serving other faiths. Mr. Jenkins will emerge as the higher-ranking "bishop," as it were, the statutory and faithful keeper of the sheep entrusted to his care. Jenkins, Lewis, Ball, and Dai Great-coat (to be introduced later) bear special weight for Jones and deserve special attention. Battles might be won and lost in the formal strategies conceived at General

Headquarters; Jones's Muse recognizes another system of values and rewards.

Part 1 is, then, properly introductory of the poem's important characters. This is the Royal Welsh Regiment, 55th battalion, "B" Company, No. 7 Platoon; it is on the move on a Friday in November 1915 from the staging grounds in England to the French coast. It moves as efficiently as might be hoped, given the rawness of the recruits who are entrained in cattle cars to be ferried across the English Channel and find themselves, on Sunday, "exposed and apprehensive in this new world" (p. 9). Their exposure and concomitant apprehension will be heightened progressively as the poem proceeds to the July apocalypse which draws relentlessly closer. Private Ball, absent in the poem's opening lines, will, in the succeeding parts, make his presence more apparent; we do well to "take that man's name" as instructed, not because he will rise to heroic feats (on the contrary, he will be as burdened and incompetent with his rifle at the end as he is with his pack and mess-tin cover in the opening parade) but because, quite literally, he is the "geste who was on the field," in the Waste Land, "Sandbag Alley" and environs, that is his temporary home, his parenthesis. It is not what he and his comrades do but what is done to them that will matter; this is an epic poem, if epic poem indeed it is, with a palpable difference.

V   *Part 2*

"Chambers Go Off, Corporals Stay" is the title of Part 2, which treats the movement of the men closer to the front lines. Following King Henry's "Once more into the breach, dear friends" call to arms, the stage directions at the end of Shakespeare's *King Henry V*, Act III, Scene 1 call for "Alarum, and chambers go off." In the following scene, Corporal Bardolph, in a bawdy exchange with Nym, calls (obviously inspired by the sound of the small cannon) for penetration of another kind of breach. There are, in *In Parenthesis*, no characters who bear ready resemblance either to King Henry V, at the one extreme, or the bawdy lesser ranks. There is, to be sure, some irreverence and blasphemy, but Jones does not exploit comic scenes; the moments soon pass. There is, however, a "chamber" that goes off at the end of Part 2, and it is no mere stage direction or back-ground noise. Nor is it the occasion for levity, though there is mild comedy in the precedent spectacle of Pri-

vate Ball being reprimanded for having failed to observe all the
proprieties in the addressing of commissioned officers—Lieutenant
Jenkins, specifically. Sergeant Snell expends his "eloquence," his
"tedious flow" of abuse on Ball, and then abruptly, almost super-
naturally, the atmosphere changes, tenses.

He looked straight at Sergeant Snell enquiringly — whose eyes changed
queerly, who ducked in under the low entry. John Ball would have followed, but stood fixed and alone in the little yard — his senses highly alert,
his body incapable of movement or response. The exact disposition of
small things — the precise shapes of trees, the tilt of a bucket, the movement of a straw, the disappearing right boot of Sergeant Snell — all
minute noises, separate and distinct, in a stillness charged through with
some approaching violence — registered not by the ear nor any single
faculty — an on-rushing pervasion, saturating all existence; with exactitude, logarithmic, dial-timed, millesimal — of calculated velocity, some
mean chemist's contrivance, a stinking physicists destroying toy   (p. 24).

The terror that flies by night and by day is about to intrude itself
most intimately into the life of John Ball; ironically it is to arrive at
the very moment when, aided by the eloquence of Sergeant Snell
and the acuteness of his sensory perceptions, he is most acutely a-
ware of the Disciplines of the Wars (a phrase from *Henry V* used
frequently throughout the poem), and of physical order, shapes,
sounds, images. No clever or ironic narrative response is possible,
and Jones reaches a rare height of vitriol in the reference to the
"mean chemist" and "stinking physicist." Such language is not
common in *In Parenthesis*; indeed, the scene militates in its enactment against the possibility in fact of Jones's proposition in the
preface: that it is not easy, but perhaps desirable nonetheless, that
we might learn to feel for these "creatures of chemicals . . . a native
affection, which alone can make them magical for us"(p.xiv).
    The scene continues:

He stood alone on the stones, his mess-tin spilled spilled at his feet. Out
of the vortex, rifling the air it came—bright, brass-shod, Pandoran; with
all-filling screaming the howling crescendo's up-piling snapt. The universal world, breath held, one half second, a bludgeoned stillness. Then the
pent violence released a consummation of all burstings out; all sudden up-
rendings and rivings-through—all taking-out of vents—all barrier-break-
ing—all unmaking. Pernitric begetting—the dissolving and splitting of sol-
id things. In which unearthing aftermath, John Ball picked up his mess-tin
and hurried within; ashen, huddled, waited in the dismal straw. Behind

"E" Battery, fifty yards down the road, a great many mangolds, uproot-
ed, pulped, congealed with chemical earth, spattered and made slippery
the rigid boards leading to the emplacement. The sap of vegetables slob-
bered the spotless breech-block of No. 3 gun (p. 24).

It is one of the major set-pieces of the poem, a scene-stopper; all
other action abides this. And there is no comfort or pleasure to be
taken in the observable irony that the manmade metal device merely
churns nature's mangolds to deface and disfigure yet another artillery piece. All the attempts to "make order, for however brief a
time, and in whatever wilderness," that have characterized Part 2
to this point are rudely insulted by this "unearthing aftermath,"
this "consummation of all burstings out." Ball is not wounded —
not yet — but now he knows as closely and as intimately as is
possible the unnatural nature of the forces ranged against him.

VI   *Part 3*

The title of Part 3, "Starlight Order," is from Gerard Manley
Hopkins's poem "The Bugler's First Communion"; the line comes
from the fifth stanza:

> Frowning and forefending angel-warder
> Squander the hell-rook ranks sally to molest him;
>   March, kind comrade, abreast him;
> Dress his days to a dexterous and starlight order.

Hopkins's verse is no more paraphrasable than Jones's; however,
the poet-priest is serving to a bugler boy in regimental red his first
communion and invoking divine guardianship of the boy whose
"drift / Seems by a divíne doom chánneled." The highly liturgical
tone is continued in the opening lines, with a passage closely parallel to the Good Friday Office (Rubrics) of the Roman Catholic rite
as performed by the priest, and the whole part is laced through with
religious and biblical allusion.

For John Ball there was in this night's parading, for all the fear in it, a
kind of blessedness, here was borne away with yesterday's remoteness, an
accumulated tedium, all they'd piled on since enlistment day: a whole
unlovely order this night would transubstantiate, lend some grace to
                                                                (p. 27).

But the frustrations and discomforts of the night deny such hope or comforting rationalizing; the blessed peace that comes to Ball on night watch is attainable only in the sleep that finally overcomes him, duty, rats, and rain notwithstanding.

There are no stars in this "starlight order"; there is a moon, shielded by cloud, "yet her veiled influence illuminated the texture of that place, her glistening on the saturated fields; bat-night gloom inter-silvered where she shone on the mist drift" (p. 27). It is a night parading followed by patrol: "the dark seemed gaining on the hidden moon," and then "the clouded moon quite lost her influence." Any light comes now from field batteries, and "there's no kind light to lead." The phrase echoes Cardinal Newman's hymn, but again ironically, and the night's darkness is characterized as the "kindlier night" for what it has hidden — the debris of the wasted land. Indeed, the whole part is obsessed with, keeps coming back to, images of light and darkness; it is "the hide and seek of dark-lit light-dark," in which even the match to light a cigarette functions as a beacon. The only starlight, as in Hopkins's phrase, is contained in a "solitary star-shell," and it illumines walking shades of men, Lazarus figures in the sepulchre brightened with chloride of lime. In the darkness and mud the men lose contact, lose connection; Corporal Quilter sprawls in the mud; Ball's wet rifle sling cuts into his clavicle; water pours from his left boot as he lifts it clear of an earth wall:

> Can you see anything, sentry.
> Nothing corporal.
> '01 Ball is it, no.
> Yes corporal.
> Keep a sharp outlook sentry — it is the most
> elementary disciplines — sights at 350   (p. 52).

But there is nothing to see, and the images of the last two pages of this part have to do with feeling, touching, remembering, and hearing. The eyes have closed; that most elementary faculty, that most elementary discipline, has failed; the prayers for the serenity of a "starlight order" have been in vain.

VII *Part 4*

The waiting continues — more parades, fatigues, patrols, work-parties, guard duty. Rations of food and tobacco are dispensed to

the hungry flock; there is mail from home; a comic moment as a
Frenchman looks for his dog, Belle, in the trenches. Mostly, it's
just waiting in the rain. "King Pellam's Launde" out of Malory is
the setting in Romance, familiar to most modern readers as the
Waste Land through which the would-be blessed knights must tra-
vel. But it's "Sandbag Alley" in the present. Private Ball takes out
his book, his only book (there is room for but one in his pack), and
it is an anthology which he opens to Dunbar's "Lament for the Makaris." Again, the reference is back to late medieval times, but the
refrain of that poem, omitted in Jones's quoting of a few lines, is
ominously familiar and too close to Private Ball's realities to let
him read on: "*Timor mortis conturbat me.*" The fear of death does
indeed lie heavy upon the souls here, but one man rises to it, rises a-
bove it, in a heroic boast familiar in more ancient literature but
oddly anachronistic, it might seem, in this poem, this war, this century.

> This Dai adjusts his slipping shoulder-straps, wraps close his
> misfit outsize greatcoat—he articulates his English with an
> alien care.
>   My fathers were with the Black Prinse of Wales
> at the passion of
> the blind Bohemian king.
> They served in these fields,
> it is in the histories that you can read it, Corporal—boys
> Gower, they were—it is writ down—yes.   (p. 79).

A rude voice, perhaps anticipating from past experience that this
bardic interlude is going to be too long, attempts to bait the orator:
"Wot about Methuselum, Taffy?" But Dai is not to be stopped:

> I was with Abel when his brother found him,
> under the green tree.
> I built a shit-house for Artaxerxes.
> I was the spear in Balin's hand
>   that made waste King Pellam's land.   (p. 79).

The speech goes on for five pages, and leaves unmentioned virtually no battle site in history. The range of allusions, to include Der-
fel Gatheren, Helen Camulodunum, Brân the Blessed, Elen Lluyd-
dawc, "the Dandy Xth," is guaranteed to send any reader to the
notes at the back of the book for elucidation.

The point must be made, however, that Dai does not, in a literal sense, exist; he is the bardic, mythic voice of the Royal Welsh regiment, of the mind of Lance-Corporal Lewis, "who fed on these things," and perhaps, more widely, of the universal soldier. In Part 7, the Queen of the Woods is to search for him, but he is not to be found in the field; rather he is embodied yet again in the mythic hosts of fresh reserves going on to battle.

His speech, oration, is a magnificent set piece of learned braggadocio, wide-ranging in its allusions to conflicts from the beginning of time to the death of Christ, almost baroque in its ornate, lavish construction. To argue that it is wholly unrealistic that a private soldier could command such breadth of learning, such vocabulary, or that the men would listen to it, let alone understand it, is quite irrelevant. A more serious objection has been raised by some critics, however, and it is one that goes right to the core of the book. Is Jones, in allowing Dai Greatcoat this forum, endorsing the warrior ethic? Is he saying it can and does endure and apply to what is, in most readers' conception, a foully conceived, foully conducted, foully sustained, modern war? The answer must, I think, lie in this. Just as Jones is not, in his words, writing a "war book," neither is he writing, explicitly, an antiwar book. Words from the preface come back: he is trying to shape in words his own experience of this war, and simultaneously making a "perpetual showing" forth of all wars. His aim is to be inclusive, not reductive or exclusive, and one with this boast is the explicit tirade against the "mean chemist" and "stinking physicist," the pity of the deaths, the bleeding, and finally the peaceable offices of the Queen of the Woods. There is savage antiwar irony aplenty, especially in Part 7: "Nothing is impossible nowadays my dear if only we can get the poor bleeder through the barrage and they take just as much trouble with the ordinary soldiers you know and essential-service academicians can match the natural hue and everything extraordinarily well" (p. 176).

Captain Cadwalladr and a new "green-gilled corporal" will appear in Part 7 as "hawks" to complement this Dai Greatcoat, as will the new wave of reserves. But it is Jenkins, Ball, and Lewis (and the gentle Roman Catholic priest in his garden) who speak, in their bodies, their sensitivities, for David Jones. He will not have it that the slain "died as men before their bodies died," and it is in the honoring of that tradition that Jones accords them this heroic model from the past. This indeed is the tradition of war poetry

from Homer to Malory and Shakespeare that Jones works so carefully; and in the case of the latter, King Henry V is the most
humane of all warrior-kings in his concern for the men. It is the
characteristic of King Arthur which Jones will most honor in the
"The Sleeping Lord" and "The Hunt." The tradition of heroism,
the tradition of gentle care for the human sacrifices, might not,
indeed does not, justify the sacrifice for modern sensibilities, but
might be seen to redeem it *ex post facto*.

VIII   *Part 5*

Part 5, "Squat Garlands for White Knights," draws on Lewis
Carroll (an unlikely source, at first glance) for the White Knight
who engages in a Punch and Judy joust with the villainous Red
Knight before delivering Alice safe to her destination and imminent
coronation as Queen. One measure of the success of Jones's poem
might well lie in how it modifies one's perception on rereading
these sources; with the imposition of the trench tactics and geography of the 1914–1918 War on to the chessboard, dialogue such
as this takes on a quite different quality.

> "It was a glorious victory, wasn't it?" said the White Knight as he came
> up panting.
> "I don't know," Alice said doubtfully. "I don't want to be anybody's
> prisoner. I want to be a Queen."
> "So you will, when you've crossed the next brook," said the White
> Knight. "I'll see you safe to the end of the wood — and then I must go
> back, you know. That's the end of my move."[5]

And "squat garlands," modified from Hopkins's "garlanded in
squat and surly steel" in his poem "Tom's Garland," when used by
Jones specifically to describe the antishrapnel helmets, again invites
grim, ironic contrast to Carroll's strangely helmeted White Knight.

Part 5 is again an account of waiting, but things are starting to
stir. It rains still, but now it is warm, steamy rain. There is small
talk, small actions; leisure time in the local *estaminet* (Alice's); military decorations and promotions (Quilter becomes Sergeant, Private Watcyn gets a stripe, Jenkins gets his full lieutenancy); Sunday
services, intramural soccer and entertainment, inspections, routines. Action now, at the front though behind the front lines, becomes more purposive; the pace quickens; there is less time for

musing or prolonged poetic set speeches. Orders are barked; company runners stir about with their messages; there is an ominous rollcall.

More grimly, there is death — close at hand. Jones does not elaborate; it seems to occur almost *en passant*; nobody seems monstrously upset by it. It is almost the expected (unlike the shell-burst in Part 2 that so unnerved Private Ball):

They came out to rest after the usual spell. The raid had been quite successful; an identification had been secured of the regiment opposite, and one wounded prisoner, who died on his way down; '75 Thomas, and another, were missing; Mr. Rhys and the new sergeant were left on his wife; you could see them plainly, hung like rag-merchants' stock, when the light was favourable; but on the second night after, Mr. Jenkins's patrol watched his bearers lift them beyond their parapets. Private Watcyn was recommended for a decoration, and given a stripe; the Commanding Officer received a contratulatory message thrugh the usual channels (p. 106).

Two aspects of this treatment need to be noted: first, the almost offhand, parenthetical way in which the deaths are reported; and second, the light irony that informs the closing lines. Far from the abrasive, consonantal language, contorted syntax, and the esoteric allusions of the set pieces described earlier, here Jones deliberately underplays his material. These are the battalion's first heroes, also its first losses, first visible deaths. And it is not a pleasant sight. But an excess of sentiment or emotion or pity would at this stage be gratuitous; there will be, in Part 7, ample opportunity, if that is the right word, to be graphic, to weep, to pray. These deaths occur on the fringe of the poem's chosen concerns; namely, those characters who by this time we have come to recognize, to know, perhaps even to care about. Therein lies the reason for the prosaic and dispassionate tone of the quoted passage, tinged but faintly with the private's recognition of misplaced acclaim in the last line.

All waits; all is in abeyance; there is no serious talk of a future — well, grim hope, perhaps, for a "cushy one," a wound serious enough to have one sent home, but not debilitating. Nothing lasts long, not even in the present: Private Watcyn's stripe is removed quickly enough — a charge of drunkenness. The fruits of valor under fire are short-lived. Lt. Jenkins can enjoy his celebratory parcel from Fortnum and Mason for now; it helps him to forget the loss of his friend Rhys, but Jenkins will himself soon be dead. Celebrations are for the moment, not in anticipation of tomorrow. Mr. Jenkins "felt an indifference to the spring offensive," and he had reasons. Part 5 ends with an ominous echo from *The Song of Roland*: "Now in this hollow between the hills was their place of rendezvous" (p. 131).

IX   *Part 6*

Part 6, "Pavilions and Captains of Hundreds," echoing, says Jones in his notes, Malory and the Old Testament, brings all into readiness for the assault. Rumor flies; extra runners are pressed into service; the artillerymen of both sides pound the terrain monotonously. Private Ball takes advantage of a brief respite to meet his closest friends; it is a rare occasion. They watch, they talk on the grassy knoll.

> They talked of ordinary things. Of each one's friends at home; those friends unknown to either of the other two. Of the possible duration of the war. Of how they would meet and in what good places afterwards. Of the dissimilar merits of Welshmen and Cockneys. Of the diverse virtues of Regular and Temporary officers. Of if you'd read the books of Mr. Wells. Of the poetry of Rupert Brooke. Of how you really couldn't very well carry more than one book at a time in your pack. Of the losses of the Battalion since they'd come to France... Of whether anyone would ever get leave and what it would be like if you did. Of how stripes, stars, chevrons, specialisations, jobs away from the battalion, and all distinguishing marks were better resisted for as long as possible. Of how it were best to take no particular notice, to let the stuff go over you, how it were wise to lie doggo and to wait the end   (p. 140).

It is almost a picnic, a version of a pastoral. Intimate comradeship is of a more hopeful order than the "Disciplines of the Wars"; there may be a future yet. "End" can still mean, in this context, the end of duration, the end of the war.

   Then abruptly all are summoned back to their respective duties. Private Ball shares his seed-cake, the last touch of home in a parcel from his aunt; it "cannot conveniently be taken" with pack, rifle, ammunition, and four grenades. They move up, then back, then up again — past the graveyard for the "civvy dead who died in the Lord with *Libera nos* and full observance"; for the rest "shovelled just into surface soil like dog — with perhaps an *Our Father* said if it was extra quiet"; past where the battery mules lie dead: "their tough clipt hides that have a homely texture flayed horrid to make you weep, sunk in their servility of chain and leather. There had been only time to shove them just out of the road" (p. 149). The view of the burial grounds again is brief, and there is no comfort to be taken in rites or prayers *post mortem*; the visible corpses of the mules, packhorses in service of the Machine, are grim reminders of what a soldier is, living, and might well be tomorrow, dead.

"The next day they saw, for the first time, infantry go forward to assault." Private Ball and his comrades are spectators still, but hardly disinterested; only their interminable duties in the interminable trenches keep them from too much wondering. And during the night they are moved; they are next.

X   *Part 7*

It is in Part 7, "The Five Unmistakable Marks," that the poem is best. This is not to praise the heroism or to lament the debacle, but to laud artistry of the highest order. This is magnificent poetry, dramatically the fitting climax to the preceding action, and in its own right a memorable spectacle, or experience, of man going to war. It is in Part 7, too, that the themes of man in chaos in pursuit of order, by whatever means available, come to the fore. The themes come not as military or liturgical or mythological abstractions, but in the person of the fighting man.

The order so carefully set up in Part 1 lies by the poem's end in ruins. Of those introduced at that time, Lillywhite, Jenkins, Quilter, and Lewis are dead; so too are others brought more sketchily, and later, into the narrative — Wastebottom, Talacryn, Bobby Saunders. The Welshman Watcyn, devotee of football scores and foil in spiritual depth to Lance-Corporal Lewis, has so far escaped death or injury, but there is no evident, conscious manipulation by Jones of who dies, or who, it might be said in some sense, deserves to die. All are under a "like condemnation"; death is random, the great leveler, and lowers with equal lack of discrimination (she is a whore) the priestly Lewis and newly promoted Quilter:

But sweet sister death has gone debauched today and stalks on this high ground with strumpet confidence, makes no coy veiling of her appetite but leers from you to me with all her parts discovered.
　　By one and one the line gaps, where her fancy will — howsoever they may howl for their virginity she holds them   (p. 162).

"The Five Unmistakable Marks" takes its title from Lewis Carroll's *The Hunting of the Snark*, though to what immediate purpose used here is not self-evident. The enumerated characteristics
by which one can recognize the Snark bear no relevance here; more
importantly, Jones refers perhaps to the wounds of Christ on the
cross and the five senses by which man may be judged to be alive or
capable of surviving. A more vivid and horrific image drawn from
Carroll is a description of '72 Morgan's severed head: "its visage
grins like the Cheshire cat / and full grimly" (p. 180). There is
grim foreboding, not hope, as Part 7 opens under the aegis of in-
stitutionalized religion, with lines in Latin from the *Tenebrae*, ex-
tinguishing of the candles in memory of the Crucifixion, for Good
Friday. It is four o'clock in the morning, an "impossible hour";
the men wait:

> And this is the manner of their waiting:
> Those happy who had borne the yoke
> who kept their peace
> and these other in a like condemnation
> to the place of a skull   (p. 154).

Some die early from the shelling: Wastebottom, disciplined even
in death, who "maintained correct alignment with the others, face
down, and you never would have guessed" (p. 158); Talacryn, who

> . . . leaps up & says
> he's dead, a-slither down the pale face — his limbs a-girandole
> at the bottom of the nullah,
> but the mechanism slackens, unfed
> and he is quite still
> which leaves five paces between you and the next live one to
> the left   (p. 158).

The remainder wait, then move up slowly from where the unnamed
guide had left them. The Welsh in the Royal Welch Regiment sing
"Jesu lover of my soul" to the Aberystwyth melody; the "rash-lev-
ied" are silent. The Lazarus figures rise from one sepulcher to confront another:

> Everyone of these, stood, separate, upright,
>   / above ground,
>   blinkt to the broad light
>   risen dry mouthed from the chalk

> vivified from the Nullah without commotion
> and to distinctly said words,
> moved in open order and keeping admirable
> / formation
> and at the high port position
> walking in the morning on the flat roof of the
> / world
> and some walked delicately
> sensible of their particular judgment   (p. 162).

They move at command, at the "effective word," which is not at all the same thing as the unmentionable "efficacious word" earlier. The command is hierarchic, authoritarian, wholly utilitarian, with none of the redeeming value that inheres in the privates' curse. They move into No-Man's Land, where men are alien beings, where they are no longer men but pawns:

> Across upon this undulated board of verdure chequered
> bright
> when you look to left and right
> small, drab, bundled pawns severally make effort
> moved in tenuous line
> and if you looked behind — the next wave came
> slowly, as successive surfs creep in to dissipate on flat shore;
> and to your front, stretched long laterally,
> and receded deeply,
> the dark wood   (p. 165).

Lance-Corporal Lewis, who had dispensed in his appointed time the salvation of sustaining rations and tobacco, is already dead. His mode of death, his manner of dying, his time of death are unknown (there is no forced narrative tidiness in Part 7). He is sung *in absentia*:

> No one to care there for Aneirin Lewis spilled there
> who worshipped his ancestors like a Chink
> who sleeps in Arthur's lap
> who saw Olwen-trefoils some moonlighted night
> on precarious slats at Festubert,
> on narrow foothold on le Plantin march —
> more shaved he is to the bare bone than
> Yspaddadan Penkawr   (p. 155).

Mr. Jenkins's death is appropriately sacrificial. In advance of his platoon, he who had ministered to his "armed bishopric" in earlier, quieter days, is hit, and goes down in a grotesque attitude of prayer:

> He makes the conventional sign
> and there is the deeply inward effort of spent men who would
> make response for him,
> and take it at the double.
> He sinks on one knee
> and now on the other,
> his upper body tilts in rigid inclination
> this way and back;
> weighted lanyard runs out to full tether,
> > swings like a pendulum
> > and the clock run down   (p. 166).

Dai Great-coat, Welsh singer of heroic boasts, is dismembered, and dying cries in agony to all the maternal muses:

> . . . mother earth
> she's kind: Pray her hide you in her deeps
> she's only refuge against
> this ferocious pursuer
> terribly questing.
> Maiden of the digged places
> > let our cry come unto thee.
> *Mam*, moder, mother of me
> Mother of Christ under the tree
> reduce our dimensional vulnerability to
> > / the minimum —
> cover the spines of us
> let us creep back dark-bellied where he
> > / can't see
> don't let it.
> There, there, it can't, won't hurt — nothing
> shall harm my beautiful   (p. 177).

But there are others to lead: Sergeant Quilter, shouting encouragement and taking over from Mr. Jenkins, is all efficiency for the moment — till he too dies. And for the "better discipline of the living," a newly returned, unnamed, "green-gilled corporal, / returned last Wednesday / from some Corps sinecure," brings new methods of exhortation, "for Christ knows he must persuade old sweats with more than sewn-on chevrons" (p. 172). Private Watcyn survives in hand-to-hand bayonet combat and even remembers to "halloo the official blasphemies." But the company has yet a new leader: "Captain Cadwaladr is come to the breach full of familiar blasphemies. He wants the senior private — the front is half-right and what whore's bastard gave the retire and: Through on the flank my arse." It is evident that "Captain Cadwaladr restores / the Excellent Disciplines of the Wars" (p. 181).

For the dead, or for some of them at least, there are the posthumous comforts of institutional religion. Father Larkin is seen administering last rites as it was predicted he should do, but with what efficacy we do not know: "But why is Father Larkin talking to the dead?" The final signigicant rites are those conducted by the Queen of the Woods on those, German, English, and Welsh alike, who have fallen within her territory.

The Queen of the Woods has cut bright boughs of various flowering.
　These knew her influential eyes. Her awarding hands can pluck for each their fragile prize.
　She speaks to them according to precedence. She knows what's due to this elect society. She can choose twelve gentle-men. She knows who is most lord between the high trees and on the open down...　　(p. 185).

It is a select but still representative company that she chooses so to honor, this "July noblesse" of the fallen: six Germans, six Britons including Mr. Jenkins, including, yes, "that swine Lillywhite." She has a special wreath reserved for Dai Great-coat, but "she can't find him anywhere." But "she knows who is most lord," and it is Aneirin Merddyn Lewis, to whom she carries "a rowan sprig, for the glory of Guenedota. You couldn't hear what she said to him, because she was careful for the Disciplines of the Wars" (p. 186). She is the eternal Earth Mother — Nature, Madonna, mother, *moder*, *mam*; and her embrace brings peace, a new kind of mythic order in chaos. Her rites replace those of the military, complement and supersede those of the liturgy. But she exists only for the dead.

There is still Private Ball, wounded in the leg. Not rainwater but blood this time flows into his boot. This very gentil knight, reader of poetry, grateful recipient of a parcel from his aunt in Norwood, bestower of matches without proper ceremony to Mr. Jenkins, friend of Olivier, the signaler, and another unnamed bosom companion; believer in lying low, staying out of trouble; of unnotable prosaic name to which is attached that other, defining identification, his serial number; suffering soldier trying vainly to stem the gut wound of the comrade fallen beside him as they dig frantically — for him, it has come to this. His rifle makes special claims of him; he weighs carefully its value, its virtues, its merits in memory, in drill, but has finally to discard it. It is his albatross, his "Mariner's white oblation."

> Marry it man! Marry it!
> Cherish her, she's your very own.
>   Coax it man coax it — it's delicately and ingeniously made—it's an instrument of precision — it costs us tax-payers, money — I want you men to remember that. . .
> You know her by her bias, and by her exact error at 300, and by the deep scar at the small, by the fair flaw in the grain, above the lower sling-swivel —
> but leave it under the oak

Alone now, enemy, friend, the Queen of the Woods busy all about him, he can call on none of the disciplines or customs of war, religion, or Earth Mother. Instinct and the remnant of good sense tell him to crawl to a spot where stretcher-bearers can find him, but there is no assurance of rescue. He can only

> Lie still under the oak
> next to the Jerry
> and Sergeant Jerry Coke   (p. 187)

and listen to the tread of new platoons going on to war, new Welsh troops reincarnated from the hosts of Oeth and Annoeth. Not a "hero," a giant among men; not, like his namesake, the firebrand radical priest who was executed in the Peasants' Revolt some five centuries earlier, a "martyr" — for all the rhetoric, poetic splendor, "remythologizing" that has attended his brief parenthesis, he is finally the private soldier as casualty, as victim.

In Parenthesis is, as Jones intended, a "shape in words," the color, agony, humour, irony, tedium, violence, sacrament, the experience of the war "re-presented." Familiar, unfortunately, in its subject, it is unique in its telling. The art is grounded firmly in Jones's personal experience, and in language has that "necessary liaison with the concrete'' that Jones so admired in Malory. The result abides quibblings and demurrers about technique or "difficulty''; it is one of the most important pieces of writings to have come from the 1914 – 1918 War.

CHAPTER 4

The Anathemata

I *Introduction*

T HE *Anathemata* does not have the confined narrative structure
or the clear identification with classical epic of *In Parenthesis*;
more ambitious, certainly, than that work, it attempts something
approaching the whole cultural history of the British Isles. "What I
have written has no plan, or at least is not planned," Jones writes;
"if it has a shape it is chiefly that it returns to its beginning" (*A*,
p. 33). To read it is to engage, in a rare, esoteric way, from a most
learned and demanding tutor, in a course in Western Civilization,
which is something other than learning the sites of famous battles
in Greece and being able to recite, in order, the rulers of Rome.and
the kings and queens of England. Ideally, is is to discover via surviving art and artifact and written word, and with application of all
the modern insights and methods of literary study, anthropology,
comparative religion, and linguistics, the essential human heritage
that is ours. "All must be safely gathered in," Jones writes in "The
Myth of Arthur" essay (*E&A*, p. 243), and this poem is such a
gathering, informed by a selecting and questioning speculative
mind. The whole gesture of the poem, its whole rhetoric, is in the
way of a question, or the putting, as it were, of a proposition. It
lacks, deliberately, that purposeful grounding in experience, that
kind of "necessary liaison with the concrete" that so informed *In
Parenthesis*; in *The Anathemata* the intimate bodily apprehension
of the trench experiences gives way to intellectual and spiritual
musings and probings of the "Real Presence," as it were, of the
Roman Mass.

Even with the aid of the preface and the "apparatus," *The
Anathemata* remains for most a most difficult poem. Its diffi-

74

culties, or challenges, are obvious to any reader who opens the book at random. Footnotes are lavish; they are prominently (if conveniently) displayed at the bottom of the page, where possible; in other instances they run to occupy a page and more in their own right. The thirty-four-page preface appears a little foreboding; seven of the nine illustrations are inscriptions in Latin. There is a total of 244 pages, which is a forbidding number for most twentieth-century readers of poetry. And there is the appearance of the poem on the page, seemingly the freest of free verse, with odd, irregular line length, and some prose narrative interspersed. The language is always demanding; not only are there words taken intact from Latin, Greek, German, Anglo-Saxon, and Welsh, but there are also words in English that are hardly commonplace. (For Auden the essential "source" was the complete Oxford English Dictionary; it is a work the reader of David Jones is well advised to keep at hand.) The allusions, even when elucidated by footnote, are rare and esoteric: Padarn Red Pexa, Urbigena, Davy Gatheren, for example. Parentheses abound; the idiom of the unlettered collides with, is interspersed with, Church Latin; syntax frequently needs working out if the sense is to be grasped. And finally, Jones advises his reader that "you won't make much sense of one bit unless you read the lot" (p. 33).

The poem is partially autobiographical in that it is composed of the meandering thoughts, the persistent, groping questions of a mind very much like and to be identified with David Jones's. "In a sense the fragments that compose this book are about, or around and about, matters of all sorts which, by a kind of quasi-free association, are apt to stir in my mind at any time and as often as not 'in the time of the Mass' " (p. 31). The progress of that ritual provides one of the poem's unities; each prescribed gesture and act performed by the priest stirs thoughts in both the conscious, and all levels of subconscious, states of the silent observer-worshiper. Another unity is provided by the chronology of events covered by this quasi-free associative method, the history of the world from the farthest reaches of pre-history to the local history of Britain — Wales, in particular — and the promise of a redeemed future first made possible for Britain by the coming of Christianity. These larger outlines enclose, define, and carry the poem, though there are other themes and subthemes which persist throughout.

If the argument to reputable authority persuades, we have the testimony of W. H. Auden as to the poem's value:

It is certainly true that no reader is going to be able to make Mr. Jones' "now-ness" his own without taking a great deal of trouble and many re-readings of *Anathemata* [sic], and if he says: "I'm sorry, Mr. Jones is asking too much. I have neither the time nor the patience which he seems to expect me to bring to his poem," I do not know what argument one could use to convince him otherwise. I can only state my personal experience, namely, that I have found the time and trouble I have taken with *Anathemata* infinitely rewarding.[1]

The appeal is reinforced by T. S. Eliot, who suggests that if a writing is deemed to be obscure, the reader is likely the one at fault. He commends Jones for knowing more than the rest of us, and for recognizing the awesome problem of communication in this age.[2] The other point of view, charitably expressed by Howard Nemerov, says of *The Anathemata* that it is more of a museum than a poem, and of the footnotes that Jones "splendidly, unfailingly, anticipates our great ignorance, but does not care to anticipate our resistance."[3]

David Blamires has used the "museum" metaphor wholly approvingly:

I think we can see David Jones's poetry — more especially *The Anathemata* — as the creation of a museum. Not the sort of museum ... that is housed in a fusty, old building with bad lighting, indiscriminately lumped together, and poorly explained, but one that provokes unexpected enthusiasms in both the casual visitor and the informed expert, a museum in effect that is true to its etymology and is a real *mouseion*, a "sanctuary of the Muses."[4]

David Jones himself is the most reliable guide to the contents of his "museum," however, and his preface provides a useful and provocative introduction to the poem.

II   *The Preface*

The preface to *The Anathemata* is one of Jones's most important essays in its own right, to be included with "Art and Sacrament" and "The Myth of Arthur" as central to an understanding of his mind and work. Its importance lies far beyond its worth as an introduction to the poem, the "fragments of an attempted writing" that make up *The Anathemata*. For in the preface Jones gathers his crucial ideas, some of which are hinted at or reiterated and amplified in other of his essays (see the chapter on *Epoch and Artist*) concerning the nature of all art and of his own intentions and practice as a poet.

He is at some pains to make clear the significance of his title. The word suggests (it is, incidentally, accented on the third syllable) a variant plural form of "anathema," that which is forbidden, disliked intensely, cursed. As it is used by Jones in his poem, however, it is not confined to such interpretation. Jones has traced the word to other roots, and finds that it means, in other English authors and perhaps most importantly in the Gospel of St. Luke (following the story of the widow's mite) " 'goodly stones and gifts' that embellished the temple," and in Homer, to "delightful things and to ornaments." He goes on:

> So I mean by my title as much as it can be made to mean, or can evoke or suggest, however obliquely: the blessed things that have taken on what is cursed and the profane things that somehow are redeemed . . . things, or some aspect of them, that partake of the extra-utile and of the gratuitous; things that are the signs of something other, together with those signs that not only have the nature of a sign, but are themselves, under some mode, what they signify. Things set up, lifted up, or in whatever manner made over to the gods (p. 29).

For Jones the word is nearly synonymous with the Welsh *"anoeth"* or the "deposits" of one's culture, which are not necessarily, though the term might include, archaeological findings or artifacts. In the larger sense, man's "anathemata" define all that legacy of man that is his, that is he.

He discusses further the scholastic distinction between the demands of *Prudentia* and *Ars*; the former is "exercised about our intentions," our moral virtues; the latter "with the shape of the finished article"(p. 29). He is concerned to maintain important distinctions between the "maker" and the thing made, seeing the true function of the artist to be that of "maker" or resignifier of the deposits, raising up and revalidating the things that are at once blessed and cursed. The ideal *modus operandi* of the poet is to act as one who finds, gathers together, shapes, and re-presents the products of his conditioned mind's quasi-free association. Other concerns in the preface are Jones's urge to conserve the historic deposits which are our shared human heritage and from which, he laments, we have become, to our individual and to our civilization's loss, progressively more estranged. Jones insists that his poem is to be read aloud, slowly and with deliberation; he urges the importance of paying close attention to the poem's visual shape and spacing; he writes to justify the weighty annotation and footnotes, to account for his profuse borrowing of foreign-language words; he acknowledges some fifty or more writers and scholars, largely of this century, whose work has, "however obliquely, aided us to make our artefacts" (p. 36). He draws attention to the significant, root, but often overlooked meaning in a word (for example, to "edify" means to build, to set up); and he endorses the belief that the end of all art is to make a thing of beauty that gives rise to pleasure and delight in the beholder.

"The works of man," Jones writes, "unless they are of 'now' and of 'this place' can have no 'for ever' " (p. 24). The statement is clear; there are, however, two aspects to the question, one relating to the "historic situation" in which the poet finds himself and with which he must work, the other concerning the poet's attitude toward his art and his practice of that art. To work from the latter to the former: Jones is to insist on the position that the arts are something empirical. By this word he does not mean "utilitarian"; rather, he writes, "the attitude of the artist is necessarily empirical rather than speculative. 'Art is a virtue of the practical intelligence. All 'artistic' problems are, as such, practical problems. You can but cut the suit according to the cloth. For the artist the question is 'Does it?' rather than 'Ought it?' " (p. 18). In this respect the problems of the cook, the painter, the shipbuilder (Jones is fond of quoting Joyce on this art), and the poet are the same. For cookery is "subject to the same demands of the muse as is painting or any making that contrives things patient of being 'set up to the gods' " (p. 27). "And," he adds pointedly, "where artefacture is there is the muse" (p. 31). Incumbent upon all artists, working in any medium, Jones writes, is a "desire to uncover a valid sign" (p. 27). The word "uncover" is significant; Jones does not write "create" or "conceive" or "invent" or "imagine," for those words suggest a personal, a forcing, a speculative process that is invalid in that it goes beyond the "given," what is inherent in the deposits.

Art is never self-indulgence for Jones: "When the workman is dead the only thing that will matter is the work, objectively considered. Moreover, the workman must be dead to himself while engaged upon the work, otherwise, we have that sort of 'self-expression' which is as undesirable in the painter or the writer as in the carpenter, the cantor, the half-back, or the cook" (p. 12). The idea corresponds closely to that expressed by T. S. Eliot's description of the ideal poet's ideal vanishing act: "What happens is a continual surrender of himself as he is at the moment to something which is more valuable. The progress of an artist is a continual self-sacrifice, a continual extinction of personality."[5] The matter of poetry, not the method or the imagination of the poet, is what distinguishes that art from the others named; those arts, however "conditioned by and reflective of the particular cultural complex to which their practitioners belong" (p. 19), are not so concerned ultimately with, "in the principle that informs the poetic act, a something which cannot be disengaged from the mythus, deposits, *matière*, ethos, whole *res* of which the poet is himself a product" (p. 20). The function of the poet in contemporary civilization, then, is one of revalidating the ancient signs and resignifying what is unique and new matter — for example, the chemicals and methods of war in the twentieth century. (See the preface to *In Paranthesis*. In that context, "resignifying" might be a more accurate and less contentious term than "ennobling.")

Jones sums up the problem thus: "The whole complex of these difficulties is primarily felt by the sign-maker, the artist, because for him it is an immediate, day by day, factual problem. He has, somehow or other, to lift up valid signs; that is his specific task" (p. 23). And while Jones does not engage directly and by name those critics or leaders of other movements who demand propaganda, relevance, and "now-ness" of their poets, he anticipates their objections magnificently.

... We can, perhaps, diagnose something that appears as a constant in poetry by the following consideration: When rulers seek to impose a new order upon any such group belonging to one or other of those more primitive culture-phases, it is necessary for those rulers to take into account the influence of the poets as recalling something loved and as embodying an ethos inimical to the imposition of that new order. Whether the policy adopted is one of suppression or of some kind of patronage, a recognition of possible danger dictates the policy in either case. Leaving aside such political considerations as may cause such recognition under such circumstances, we may still recognize the "dangerous" element. Poetry is to be diagnosed as "dangerous" because it envokes and recalls, is a kind of *anamnesis* of, i.e. is an effective recalling of, something loved. In that sense it is inevitably "propaganda," in that any real formal expression propagands the reality which caused those forms and their content to be.... There is a sense in which *Barbara Allen* is many times more "propagandist" than *Rule Brittania*. The more real the thing, the more it will confound their politics   (pp. 21–22).

It is surprising to see antiquarian David Jones aligned with revolutionary Percy Shelley in confirming that poets are "the unacknowledged legislators of the world." But it is thus, ideally, that the "antiquarian" works his quiet revolution and confounds both the rear and the avant-garde.

In the preface Jones takes to himself the mantle of prophet, not as one who sees the future but as one who tries to claim, to reclaim, mankind for God; who properly may be said to have the function of propagating the Word, and who draws his warrant to comment on his own times, his own "civilizational situation," not from the splendor and decibel level of his rhetoric but from his acquaintance with the proper oracles, the proper "deposits." Jones shuns the title of seer or prophet himself, and prefers to liken himself and all artists to a "vicar whose job is legatine — a kind of Servus Servorum to deliver what has been delivered to him, who can neither add to nor take from the deposits.... There is only one tale to tell even though the telling is patient of endless development and ingenuity and can take on a million variant forms" (p. 35).

Jones is the first to concede that his is a lonely, perhaps even futile task. To make it work at all, to reinvigorate, for example, such commonplace words as "wood" with all the associations of the Cross, Calvary, the Passion; to invoke, by mere mention of their names, the host of associations surrounding classical and nonclassical figures in legend, history, and myth; to say nothing of the problems of conveying, via Latin, Greek, and Welsh words, for example, something that cannot be fully summed or evoked in translation, is a major burden — indeed, these considerations provide the major reason for his having to annotate and footnote his own material. In a letter to Vernon Watkins, Jones complained of all the reasons (basically, a lack of "unshared backgrounds") he "thought it *necessary* to append all those bloody notes (that people complain of so much) to *In Parenthesis* & *The Anathemata*.... But I'm becoming more & more doubtful as to the validity of this way of carrying on."[6]

In the second half of the essay Jones is concerned more directly with his making of, specifically, *The Anathemata*. There is, however, one other principle of wider application which Jones elucidates in the preface, and it deals with the relation between art and the Christian religion. And that relation involves directly the function of the artist as maker. It is a happy observation that the bread and wine offered in the recalling, the "anamnesis," of the Eucharist are not mere wheat and grapes in a natural state but things "which have already passed under the jurisdiction of the muse, being themselves quasi-artefacts" (p. 31). In this context Jones comes to a central truth which is to inform the whole poem, drawing on his extensive inquiries into art and religion to make contemporary and valid what others might see as quaint and by now irrelevant: "Where artefacture is, there is the muse, and those cannot escape her presence who, with whatever intention employ the signs of wine and bread. Something has to be made by us before it can become for us his sign who made us. This point he settled in the upper room. No artefacture no Christian religion" (p. 31). In his "Art and Sacrament" essay he goes even further; no art, no mankind. But *The Anathemata* is a devoutly religious poem, and the preface is intended finally as prologue to that poem and, by extension, to all of Jones's works, his artifacts, his deposits remade into things *sacra*, gathered and offered as the poet's Mass — not for the remission of sins but for art's sake, which is to say, for man's sake.

III   *Outline*

Any summary of the poem's contents or action is bound for failure at the outset, is bound to be reductive. Still, a brief attempt at describing or outlining the narrative or sequence might be useful to point the subject more clearly and to establish important connections and continuities. Part I, "Rite and Fore-time," begins: "We already and first of all discern him making this thing other" (p. 49), and is immediately indicative of what is to follow in that Jones refers simultaneously both to the Prayer of Consecration of the Host in the Latin Mass and, in the phrase "first of all," to man's earliest scratchings of an extrautilitarian art. The advent of man as *homo faber*, man the maker, is seen here not with reference to the Garden of Eden myth, but to the Paleolithic man of the anthropologist. There is no irreconcilable clash for Jones between science and revealed religion, and from the liturgical present tense in his poem, Jones's mind moves backwards in time to recall references to geological, mythological, anthropological, and religious testimonies to the eternal, sacramental, art-making creature that is man. The Ice Ages descend and retreat across the island of Britain and its surrounding seas, but not without a larger, divine sanction; Cronos is said to observe the rhetoric of the Mass, "*frangit per medium*," as "he breaks his ice like morsels, for the therapy and

fertility of the land-masses'' (p. 69). "Man-hands" of nation or
name yet unknown "god-handled the Willendorf stone" and this
first known sculpture, the "Venus of Willendorf," "her we de-
clare" (p. 60). And "see how they run, the juxtaposed forms,
brighting the vaults of Lascaux" (p. 60). These earliest artworks
point to and prefigure the central artwork "when we make the recalling of him / daily, at the Stone" (p. 81) in the celebration of the
Eucharist. That distinct act informs all that precedes as well as suc-
ceeds it; and it is the central axle, tree, keel, on which the poem is to
revolve, be supported or "lifted up," held together, and moved.

Part II, "Middle-Sea and Lear-Sea," charts graphically the voyage of the earliest Roman discoverers of the island of Britain from
the Mediterranean to their first sighting, and perhaps berthing, at
Land's End. I say "perhaps" because Part II ends with the question, "Did he berth her? / and to schedule?" (p. 108), while in
Parts III and IV other possible first landing sites, at the Isle of
Wight or London, are also given as possibilities. More likely, however, they serve as subsequent stops. Jones is dealing with an event
first told of in prehistories or legend, hence the questioning; he has
no firsthand diary or verifiable source that would provide undis-
puted evidence. There is also close correlation between Hector and
Christ, Virgil and the prophet Isaiah, as Jones brings together the
language of the *Aeneid* and the prophetic book of the Old
Testament to foreshadow the Crucifixion; the sailor in the crow's
nest who sings out as he sights land is characterized as the "close-
cowled . . . solitary cantor" who cries out his "versicle" (p. 103):
the priest as lookout. Jones's passion for specificity of detail is
noted in his use of compass points and latitudinal/longitudinal
references; his passion for the local language in specifying geographical place names: "all the way b'star and day / across the
mare [Latin] / over the *See* [German] / to go to *Dis* [Greek] in
Lear's sea [Celtic] / matlos [slang derived from French *matelot* —
sailor] of the maiden [English]" (p. 104) — the last ultimately to be
associated specifically, of course, with the Virgin Mary, to whom
these mariners of pre-Christian days might be said to pray. But it is
a crew of mixed racial and religious origin, and the prayer in its
larger sense is to "you many that are tutelar" (p. 105) — including
Phoebe, Artemis, Cythera, and so on. Jones's Blessed Mother ex-
cludes none.

There is the low idiom of "Wot'ld you do with the bleedin'
owners" (p. 104), Jones's anachronistic insertion of a variant of

the familiar "drunken sailor" sea shanty; and the further deliberate anachronism of "And us marines, remember us / as belong to y'r panzer'd lover" (p. 105), to relate military men of the twentieth century's wars to their Roman predecessors or counterparts. The point is, of course, that for Jones the word "anachronism" can have no meaning, certainly none that is pejorative. Clio, Muse of History, is "apt to be musing" without regard to chronology. Jones's larger concerns are for

> The adaptations, the fusions
> the transmogrifications
> but always
> the inward continuities
> of the site
> of place   (p. 90).

Part III, "Angle-Land," is very short and inquires further where the boat landed, what peoples were already there, what languages they spoke, what rites they performed. Jones's multilingual inquiries read, purposefully though no doubt vexingly to some, as "Did he strike soundings off Vecta Insula? / or was it already the gavelkind *igland*?" (p. 110); or was it

> Past where the ancra-man, deeping his holy rule
> in the fiendish marsh
> at the *Geisterstunde*
> on *Calangaeaf* night
> heard the bogle-*baragouinage*.
> Crowland-*diawliaidd*
> *Waelisc*-man lingo speaking?
> or Britto-Romani gone *diaboli?*   (p. 112)

as he pursues his passion for the localities and their particularities of name. The passage quoted is amply "translated," as it were, by Jones in his notes; a useful prose paraphrase is fortuitously provided by Joseph Conrad as he has his own ancient mariner, Charlie Marlow, ponder on times past as he gazes up the Thames estuary prior to telling his tale of Kurtz in *Heart of Darkness.*

"I was thinking of very old times, when the Romans first came here, nineteen hundred years ago — the other day.... Imagine the feelings of a commander of a fine — what d'ye call 'em? — trireme in the Mediterranean, ordered suddenly to the north; run overland across the Gauls in a hurry; put in charge of one of these craft the legionaries — a wonderful lot of handy men they must have been, too — used to build.... Imagine him here — the very end of the world, a sea the colour of lead, a sky the colour of smoke, a kind of ship about as rigid as a concertina — and going up this river with stores, or orders, or what you like. Sandbags, marshes, forests, savages — precious little to eat fit for a civilized man, nothing but Thames water to drink. No Falernian wine here, no going ashore. They were men enough to face the darkness....[7]

Conrad's purposes are self-evidently other than David Jones's; what Conrad evokes by description, for all its splendor, is still but a momentary recalling, characterized by its very unspecificity. "Imagine him here," writes Conrad; for David Jones the gesture is: Yes, he was here; we know it in our bones, our language, our religion, in our history and our present.

Or, asks Part IV, "Redriff" (an abbreviation for Rotherhithe), did he make the Thames estuary? Further, did he meet Eb Bradshaw of Princes Stair (the allusions are important not only to the center of shipping in London Pool and just any mast-and-block maker but to the residence and profession of Jones's maternal grandfather)? After the second question, this part becomes a short monologue by Eb Bradshaw, a master craftsman and carpenter who is unwilling to expedite — "we scamp no repairs here" — and the impatient captain is advised to wait his turn: "tell the old Jason: / As sure as I was articled, had I the job of mortisin' the beams to which was lashed and roved the Fault in all of us, I'ld take m' time and set that aspen transom square to the Rootless Tree" (p. 121). The allusions to the Fall and the Cross are perhaps self-evident; they are worth noting early, however, because Jones already has identified and will further link the mast of the ship with the Cross, "that quivering elm on which our salvation sways," to the point that it is the major recurrent motif throughout the poem. The impatient captain's "got / till the Day o' Doom / to sail the bitter seas o' the world" (p. 121).

Part V, "The Lady of the Pool," begins by asking further if this captain has toured London, its twenty-six wards, its churches, and if so, did he hear the call of the Cockney lavender girl? Had he heard it, this is what he would have heard, and this book, the longest of the eight that make up *The Anathemata*, is given over to her monologue. No ordinary lavender girl she, however, witness her solicitation:

> *Who'll try my sweet prime lavendula*
> *I cry my introit in a* Dirige-*time*
> *Come buy for summer's weeds, threnodic stalks*
> *For in Jane's ditch Jack soon shall white*
> *   / his earliest rime*   (p. 125)

She changes shape and is variously to be identified in her now erudite, now slangy voice with Helen of Troy, the Lady of the Lake, the mermaids, Elen Monica, Flora Dea, Iphigenia at Aulis, and a host of female figures from mythology; she is veritably the queen of this "Matriarch's Isle." Also she has met virtually every sailor who ever called in London (and a lot of those who never did, literally); has sold lavender to them, laughed and loved with them:

> Dont eye *me*, captain
> don't eye *me*, 'tis but a try-out and very much betimes:
> For we live before her time   (p. 146).

No virgin she, yet as voice for all women of all time in the poem, she asserts fecundity, power, and the primacy of a force of "deep fluvial doings" that can restore life to the dead King Arthur: "You never know, captain: / What's under works up" (p. 164).

Part VI is titled "Keel, Ram, Stauros," for ship, weapon of war-making, and redeeming cross, all products of the carpenter's art, and asks further of the itinerant captain where he went and whom he met. At the end of this book, a short but important one in its unifying of motifs and images, the captain is recognized, if only tentatively, as savior: "He would berth us / and to schedule" (the question of Part II is answered) and identified too with Coleridge's Ancient Mariner: "Pious, eld, bright-eyed / *marinus*. / Diocesan of us" (p. 182), who, by the end of his tale, has learned how to pray (lest we had forgotten the Mass to which the whole argosy of voyage to date in the poem is but an extended annotation).

Part VII is "Mabinog's Liturgy," the bard's prayer, bringing us simultaneously back to "the present moment of the past": "Our van / where *we* come in: / not our advanced details now, but us and all our baggage" (p. 190). The captain, protagonist, has become, as it were, now the priest and the High Priest, Christ, and the voice of this book is that of the poet (bard, mabinog) intent on anamnesis, reliving the Nativity and the Crucifixion, specifying it in time and place. The meditation is interrupted by a chorus of weird sisters from *Macbeth*, "malkins three" from Virgil, who

speak of their conversion from pagandom to adoration of the Babe
and His Mother. They testify to the power of womankind, her
place in the eternal scheme of things:

Sisters, not so jealous! *Someone* must be chosen and forechosen — it
stands to reason ! After all there should be solidarity in women. No great
thing but what there's a woman behind it, sisters. Begetters of all huge
endeavour we are. The Lord God may well do all without the aid of man,
but even in the things of god a woman is medial — it stands to reason

(p. 214).

Part VIII, "Sherthursdaye and Venus Day," draws close to the
celebration of the Eucharist on Maundy Thursday, preceding the
days of the Passion, in which the poet looks plainly at the priest
performing his holy office and explains:

> He does what is done in many places
> what he does other
>   he does after the mode
> of what has always been done   (p. 244).

True, the poem is to end with the question mark still in evidence;
but here it is wholly a rhetorical question, containing its own answer.

> What did he do other
>   recumbent at the garnished supper?
> What did he do yet other
>   riding the Axile Tree?   (p. 244).

There is an order, a serenity, in Part VIII that is born of clear
recognition; the meditations having moved "down the traversed
history paths" (p. 228) forward from the initial "rite and fore-
time" and backward from "this sagging present and wasted close"
(p. 49), all attention rivets itself on the Cross at Calvary. The
poem's beginning, center, end — but more importantly its continuity — are established beyond any possibility of misunderstanding.

IV   *Celtic to Christian*

Literary criticism cannot stop with summary or description of contents, nor it is possible or profitable in this context merely to add to the learned annotation already provided by Jones and his critics and commentators. Nor is it sufficient merely to affirm or deny the validity or worth of Jones's Welshness and Catholic subscription. "If I thought the book was only for Welsh Roman Catholics," wrote T. S. Eliot, "I should not have the impudence to talk about it."[8] Indeed if the work were so restricted in its loves it could draw only about 5 percent of Wales's fewer than three million inhabitants. Such readers might indeed have a head start in natural or native sympathy and in spontaneous recognition of the multiple allusions; the rest will just have to learn from the beginning, preassured that their time and effort will be amply rewarded. Clearly, it is the whole of human history and prehistory as perceived and experienced by Western man that is Jones's province in *The Anathemata*. In intention and performance the poem will withstand criticism's severest, most demanding tests of high seriousness and moral exactitude. In intention and performance it is governed, however, by the restrictions of its religious and national bias or authorial predispositions. To say this is not to use the word "restrictions" pejoratively; it is to isolate for further examination the conditioning forces working on, in, and through the poem that Jones, before anyone, would acknowledge. What makes *The Anathemata* significant, and significantly different, are two determining factors: first, it is informed and defined throughout by a Christian, or, more exclusively, a Roman Catholic point of view; and second, Jones is writing as a Welshman, a London Welshman.

The cross and the unnamed priest at the altar occupy the sacramental center of the poem; the island of Britain and the poet, David Jones himself, occupy the geographical center. Standing, as it were, with one foot in Wales, one in London, is the poet, who is celebrant, or at least silent and attentive observer, at the Mass. He is a citizen of the British Isles, "a person whose perceptions are totally conditioned and limited by and dependent upon his being indigenous to this island," and further, he is "a Londoner, of Welsh and English parentage, of Protestant upbringing, of Catholic subscription" (p. 11). Not all of this could legitimately be inferred from the words of the poem itself, perhaps, but then that's why Jones wrote the preface. The significance of both Catholic and British allegiances is, for Jones, inextricably bound together. These are, in one sense, limiting allegiances, or would be for a lesser mind. But for Jones they are invoked not in the name of parochialism or jingoism but because they are inescapable; they define and enclose his "deposits," those mysteries that are his to uncover and revalidate, his mysteries in need of a new sign. They are to be his offering, his "anathemata."

The Welsh aspects of the poem are central, though perhaps not as all-pervasive as in *In Parenthesis*, and are given fullest expression in Part VII, "Mabinog's Liturgy," where the bard's repertoire or *mabinogi* is made liturgical, thus fusing the elements of Welsh legend, which is paganism adulterated in large degree by Christianity, and the orthodox Christian faith of Rome. The speaker's bias is plain; it is "our Gwenhwyfar," with "our" designating the all-British claim on the localized Welsh rendering of the name of Arthur's queen. The whole Arthurian cycle is invoked repeatedly throughout, commencing with the title-page inscription: "*This prophecie Merlin shall make / for I live before his time.*" The lines are characteristically circular and ambiguous in origin (*King Lear*, III, ii, 95 — a Folio interpolation) and meaning. Arthur is the once and future king who, like Christ, will harrow Hell and rise again. In Part I, the geological movements of the "pre-Cambrian oreosheavers" (p. 67) of the Ice Age are made to direct their energies to the forming, specifically, of Mount Snowdon in Wales, where lie "dragons and old Pendragons / very bleached" (p. 68).

> Before, trans-Solway
> and from over Manannan's *moroedd,* the last debris-
> freighted floes echeloned solid from Monapia to Ynys Fôn
> discharged on Arfon *colles*
> what was cargoed-up on Grampius Mons.
> Off the "strath" into the *ystrad*
> out of the "carse" on to the *traeth.*
> Heaped amorphous
> out of Caledonia
> into Cambria
> bound for Snowdonia
> transits Cumbria   (p. 70).

The passage quoted above is detailed and dense, not to obscure but rather to illuminate and specify. The ice moves southward, a kind of cargo, passing from the Scottish *strath* to the Welsh *ystrad*, from the *carse* to the *traeth*. The English equivalents — the familiar "vale" or "plain" or "beach" — are just not equivalents at all and are, most importantly for Jones in this instance, irrelevant and impossible. Then there is that happy conjunction which makes "pre-Cambrian" refer to the most remote time, according to geologists' time schemes, while Cambria is also an English word for Wales itself, derived from *Cymru*. (Such "accidents" are never lost on Jones.) The effect is to make all the energies of the Creation and all man's and nature's subsequent evolutionary strivings point to a spot in time, the present, in modern Britain and Wales, specifically. The coal that is the wealth and also the tragedy of modern indus-trialized Wales (cf. the sentimental title of *How Green Was My Valley*) is part of that Creation; before the coming of man "the slow estuarine alchemies had coal-blacked the green dryad-ways over the fire-clayed seat-earth along all the utile seams from Taff to Tâf" (p. 72) — that is, from border to border of the coalfield in South Wales.

The voice or tone of the poem is bardic in the traditional Welsh sense in two respects: that it is intended for oral performance and that is is celebratory of national concerns rather than personal. That Jones makes use (if not according to the strictest of the medieval Eisteddfod rules) of such Welsh poetic devices as *cynghanedd* is evident throughout; note, for example, the complex pattern of repeated and interlocking consonontal and vowel "chimes" in

> breasting the gulled grey, westing
> over wave, wind's daughter
> over billow, son of wave   (p. 99).

And a good portion of Jones's notes are intended to instruct the reader in pronunciation of the Welsh words. The overall circular, diffuse, and shifting structure is characteristically Welsh or Celtic, as Sir Thomas Parry and others have demonstrated historically.[9] Clearly *The Anathemata* has affinities with Joyce's *Ulysses*, which for all its classical order and narrative structure borrowed from the *Odyssey*, doubles in upon itself, and is more cyclical than sequen-tial. *Finnegans Wake* is, in this respect, more obviously com-parable. As Gwyn Williams describes the Welsh "model" or prece-dent: "Aneirin, Gwalchmai, Cynddelw and Hywel ab Owain were not trying to write poems that would read like Greek temples or even Gothic cathedrals, but, rather, like stone circles or the con-tour-following rings of the forest from which they fought, with hid-den ways slipping from one ring to another."[10] *The Anathemata* is, then, circular in construction, but not symmetrically so; rather it (like *Finnegans Wake*) devolves upon itself, posing riddles and puns and answering likewise. (Jones does not, however, coin words as did Joyce). The epigraph reads:

> IT WAS A DARK AND STORMY NIGHT, WE SAT BY
> THE CALCINED WALL: IT WAS SAID TO THE TALE
> TELLER, TELL US A TALE, AND THE TALE RAN THUS:
> "IT WAS A DARK AND STORMY NIGHT. ...."

Jones, "himself at the cave-mouth" (p. 66), characteristically puts the domestic and familiar into the recesses of antiquity, taking the mind back to those earliest men and women and children crouching amidst the calcined walls of caves. And in this circularity and repetition is fulfilled the promise of the epigraph and the children's plea, "Tell us a story."

Other modern writings, distinctly non-Celtic in origin — say, T. S. Eliot's *The Waste Land* and *Four Quartets* and the novels of Virginia Woolf — might be compared. The "rhythmical grumblings" of *The Waste Land* testify in fact, in their noncompletion, to the impossibility of drawing meaningful sequential order; in *Four Quartets,* the movement of the poet's mind is not chronologically progressive and "the end of all our exploring / Will be to arrive where we started / And know the place for the first time."[11] In a different way "time passes" in Virginia Woolf's *To the Lighthouse*, wherein her characters seek various ways of evoking order, seek to "make of the moment something permanent."[12] In this respect, to see Joyce the Celt as charter of post-Georgian prose-poetry and allies like Eliot and Woolf, impeccably "English" as they are, developing virtually the same methods, is to see the Celtic influence becoming again an integral and indispensable part of the mainstream of literature in English. What Joyce did for Ireland, then, David Jones has done for Wales; together they do a lot for English poetry.

In *In Parenthesis*, Jones leaned heavily on *Y Gododdin* as model, not merely for its Welshness but for its celebration, if that is the word, of a military disaster that was a forerunner of the Battle of the Somme. *The Anathemata* in one sense is more traditionally an epic poem on the model of Virgil; that is, it is concerned not with breaking down and falling apart but with raising, ennobling, and "lifting up." Christ, linked with Hector and Arthur, is more clearly a heroic figure than, say, John Ball. Note Jones's language, linking that of Virgil and the prophet Isaiah, in the following passage, as he brings Hector and Christ into one:

> Twelve hundred years
>   close on
> since of the Seven grouped Shiners
>   one doused her light.
> Since Troy fired
>   since they dragged him
>   widdershins
> without the wall.
> When they regarded him:
> his beauties made squalid, his combed gilt
>   a matted mop
> his bruised feet thonged
>   under his own wall   (p. 84).

In Christ's heroic boast as given in "Mabinog's Liturgy," attributes drawn from Taliesin, Malory, the *Mabinogion*, the Book of Isaiah, the Old English "Dream of the Rood," join with the Latin of Virgil and the Mass:

> *Alpha es et O*
>   that which
> the whole world cannot hold.
> Atheling to the heaven-king.
> Shepherd of Greekland
> Harrower of Annwn
> Freer of the Waters.
> Chief Physician and
> *dux et pontifex.*
> Gwledig Nefoedd and
> Walda of *every* land
> *et vocabitur* WONDERFUL   (pp. 207–208).

The veneration of the Virgin takes the form of a rollcall of all renowned women: Calypso, Helen, Martha, Gwenhwyfar, Selene, Helene, the weird sisters, even Marged, Mal Fay, and Mabli, "malkins three," in Part VII, "Mabinog's Liturgy." Theirs is a boast on behalf of motherhood, a hymn to matriarchy:

Even the gigantic *dynion gynt* and mighty tyrannoi of old time needs have

had mortal woman for mothers, if demi-gods or whatever father'd em —
it stand to reason ... after all, sisters, he was her *baban*   (p.214).

And for the poet, the observer, the recording mind, things come
finally clear; the Celtic cult of matriarchy, the classical female
heroines, the *Dea Matres*, and the worship of the earthly mother of
Christ are perceived as one. "Mary" she might be in England;
"Maria" in Italy; but in Wales —

> Modron our mother?
> *Ein mam hawddgar*?
> Truly!
> that we must now call MAIR   (p. 217).

V   *Dramatic Voices*

All the "voices" of *The Anathemata* bear on, dwell on, expand
upon, allude to, these central concerns, and another kind of entrance to the poem might well be to consider it, like Dylan Thomas's
Under Milk-Wood, as a "play for voices." As narrator there is
the poet — to reiterate, David Jones, Welsh-Briton,Catholic
convert, communicant, World War I veteran, antiquarian, painter,
prophet — "*Teste David cum Sibylla*," says another inscription,
linking the pagan prophetess with the poet himself, to say nothing
of the biblical and biographical reverberations in the name of
David. David Jones is always there, abstracted in that he has no
form or personal presence, and in more an enquiring than confessional mode. He speaks, he inquires, not for himself but as representative man of his generation; he says no *mea culpa*; he does not
pour out his heart in confession of sin. His voice is far less intense
than Eliot's in "Ash Wednesday," for this is not a personal quest
for salvation; it is not a private "Let my cry come unto Thee."
More accurately, it is for the poet himself a plea to let his mind
draw near. For Jones the approach to the mysteries of the human
past and contemporary presence is through art forms, not peni-
tence; and he sees the Eucharist as the supreme work of art. Thus
the informing rhetorical design of this narrator's voice and the en-
tire poem is the question mark; it is the poet in pursuit of the mysteries with intense observation and intellectual querying, commencing on the poem's second page and continuing throughout. Six of

the eight parts actually begin in this sort of interrogation; four, including the last, so conclude.

Throughout there is the other figure of the priest — "Within the railed tumulus / he sings high and he sings low" (p. 51) — performing humbly his appointed duties in celebrating the Mass. And while he employs the "groping syntax" of the Latin, his cocelebrant, the poet, speculates on all the associations that come to his mind. Properly done, all free or quasi-free association is in the nature of a question; dissimilar objects, personalities, events, ideas, references, allusions, suggest themselves and immediately give rise in the thinker to the "why?" of their juxtaposition. The relationship perceived, if only momentarily, if only in recognition of its absurdity, affords pleasure, pain, elation, disdain, whatever — but always insight. In the priest is the figure of assured, perhaps near-mechanical performance; in the mind of the poet observing him is started the whole history of Britain and her origins, the details of which proceed from questions. It is a method born of liberated concentration in a way that the instructions of Pope Pius XII seem to condemn:

It is desirable that all the faithful should be aware that to participate in the Eucharistic Sacrifice is their chief duty and supreme dignity, and that, not in an inert and negligent fashion, giving way to distractions and daydreaming, but with such earnestness and concentration that they may be united as closely as possible with the High Priest. . . . [13]

In one sense Jones may be said to be daydreaming or wool-gathering, but there is nothing "inert" or "negligent" about the product of such thought. Now there are other voices in the poem, already noted, from Clio the Muse of History to Ebenezer Bradshaw, Jones's maternal grandfather, to the Lady of the Pool, Cockney and all-motherly, to the three weird sisters of "Mabinog's Liturgy." These speak not in questions but with answers. Clio tells of the conception of the city of Rome at the loins of Mars, "the square-pushing Strider"; Ebenezer Bradshaw asserts his independence and defies the temptation to engage in hasty, uncraftsmanlike work. And as surety for his oath, even were this carpenter to be called upon to construct the Cross itself, Bradshaw invokes the Trinity Brethren, the Holy Ghost, Canute, and Proserpine.

The Lady of the Pool, crying her "*introit in a* dirige *time*," has but one question: "Who'll buy my sweet lavender?" Hers is the voice of eternal femaleness, coarse and strident at times, again

gentle and supplicant. Part VII is her monologue in which she gives
the visiting sea-captain what amounts to a local and islandwide history of the land, from the fringe areas of the Corn-Welsh (Cornwall) to the local shipping pools of London. Her performance is
also a sustained monologue on the manners and methods of her
lovers, faintly reminiscent of Molly Bloom's soliloquy. Give her an
audience and she'll recount the history of her lives and loves and
the history of the matriarchs of Britain; she is joined chorically by
the pagan "malkins three," late converts to Christianity.

These choruses and monologues are in total the strongest parts of
the poem; these speakers know all, past, present, future. They
speak without hesitation, without equivocation. Their responses
rely for effectiveness on the gesture of the initial question or problem posed by the "narrator," of course; nevertheless, the answers
go so far beyond the literal demands of the question that they are
set orations in their own right. Each speaker contributes a host of
allusive references that provide a new insight into what it means, in
the widest possible sense, to be British in the mid-twentieth century.

These voices and the tone of their exposition also serve to reas-
sure the hesitant, questioning voice of the poet. His question on the
presence of Christ himself in ancient Britain, drawing on Blake's
"And did those feet in ancient time / Walk upon England's mountains green?" momentarily brings the poet to something near despair:

> I do not know!
> I do not know!!
> I do not know what time is at
> or whether before or after
>   was it when —
> but when *is* when?

At this juncture in the poem there can be no conclusion, only the
undefined assurance:

> All we do know is
> that from before long ago he
>   sailed our *Mori Marusam*   (p. 170).

There are always more questions than answers, but the poet is persistent, and his restless mind pursues its inquiries. He receives guidance at the poem's end, and it issues in an imperative urge to retell

or reask the story. Like Coleridge's Ancient Mariner, he is appointed to retell his tale, which is, according to the preface, the only story there is to tell, patient of endless repetition. "Repetition" in the celebration of the Eucharist is of the essence: "he does what has always been done," and the closing interrogative is clearly rhetorical, its answer self-evident. To repeat:

> What did he do other
>   recumbent at the garnished supper?
> What did he do yet other
>   riding the Axile Tree?   (p. 244).

The referent of the pronoun "he" (Jones does not capitalize it) has shifted from the priest to the first "priest" that was Christ, from the present site to Jerusalem nineteen hundred years ago. The far-ranging mind has returned to the central object of its attention. Having circumnavigated the known globe and penetrated the mysteries of rite in fore-time and through the centuries, it returns to contemplate, in celebration and anamnesis, He who instituted, even as He continued, the visible art form that redeems mankind. Rhetorically we are back at the poem's beginning: "We already and first of all discern him making this thing other," where "him" refers at once to Christ at the Last Supper on Maundy Thursday, to the present priest already busily engaged, and also to man in his earliest origins as "man master-of-plastic," *homo faber* of the "Venus of Willendorf":

> But already he's at it
> the form-making proto-maker
> busy at the fecund image of her   (p. 59).

VI *Conclusion*

The Anathemata is a verse rendering of, a demonstration of, both a theory of poetry and a body of belief about the nature of man. It has that story to tell, "even though the telling is patient of endless development and ingenuity and can take on a million variant forms" (p. 35). At its widest scope that is the story of mankind on earth, his emergence from the reaches of prehistory, from rocks and caves that he decorated, as at Lascaux, adorning burial sites gratuitously, creating objects that are beautiful to an extrautile degree, and continuing, still an artmaker, to the wasted present, "at the sagging end and chapter's close." For David Jones, inextricably bound up with man's persistence as an art-making creature is the smaller story, that is potentially of infinitely wide, eternal scope, which is the "one tale to tell" of man's redemption by the gratuitous intercession of Christ on the Cross. At the center of *The Anathemata* is that cross, the "Axile Tree," "the quivering elm on which our salvation sways," itself an object of art, being wood which has passed under the hand of the carpenter, and ironically (though not accidentally) bearing upon it one who had himself been a carpenter. Christ, "Son of Mair, wife of jobbing carpenter" (p. 207), being lifted upon it validated the cross as man's artwork; Christ being lifted up made an efficacious sign, made "anathemata" of his own body. In his life and death he became man fully, says traditional Christian doctrine, while in his resurrection and ascension he became again supernatural, taking his place again as Second Person of the Trinity. For David Jones, Christ became man wholly when he broke the bread and poured the wine and said, "This is may body . . . this do in remembrance of me"

The rite of the Eucharist is then Christ's prescribed artform for remembrance of His death, and for Jones and like believers it is the Roman Catholic Church to whom the duty of caretaking and daily anamnesis is entrusted. *The Anathemata* begins with "this man so late in time, curiously surviving" handling the objects of the symbolic sacrifice — no, more than symbolic, for in the Roman Church's doctrine of transubstantiation the bread and wine actually are transformed at the moment of consecration into the body and blood of Christ. Jones's concern is to go beyond, if it is possible, the Mass as "merely" celebratory of the body and blood of Christ, and to see it as signifying the whole odyssey of the human experience on earth. Whether one believes that the events recorded in the Christian gospel actually happened or not, or whether or not he believes that Christ was the Son of God, as He claimed to be, really matters little, for Western man's whole being, his history, his ancestry, his "*res*," is wholly bound up in the myth. Jones establishes in *The Anathemata* that the art of the first Eucharist at the Last Supper redefines all preceding art, even as it was an act that with all its reverberations and implications transformed succeeding events and imparted a unique and new order to Western myth, legend, and history. The poem's last lines lead us from this present time "In the wasted land / at jackal-meet" (p. 231) to Jerusalem, and in the circular structure of the poem back again to the Creation, to the oreogenesis of foretime. While the final event referred

to is the Crucifixion, that act is to be seen as the confirmed and
eternally valid lifting up of a sign that actually resignifies events
that preceded it.

> high as Hector the Wall
> high as Helen the Moon
> who, being lifted up
> draw the West to them   (p. 56).

If the gesture of myth is finally the redemption, the only possibility of authentic meaning, in *In Parenthesis*, then *The Anathemata* may be seen as a refinement, narrowing, purification of that
solution. That is, it proposes a specific myth, that of the traditional
Christian story of Christ as redeemer of mankind; this, for Jones,
is efficacious, and not only for the dead. In *The Anathemata* there
is no Queen of the Woods giving mixed pagan-Christian consola-
tion to the fallen by bestowing garlands, but Christ vicariously, and
the priest of the Church in person, celebrating the sacrament of the
Eucharist on behalf of all mankind. *The Anathemata* celebrates
simultaneously the handiwork, mind, imagination, and soul of
man creating "monuments of its own magnificence," in Yeats's
phrase; *In Parenthesis* is the verse rendering of the concrete experience of man at war. After all, if man is distinguished from the
angels and the beasts by his ability to create art, he is distinguished
further by his lone passion for organized mass violence. *In Parenthesis* tested the military and liturgical forms of order and found
them lacking, with neither efficacy for salvation nor effectiveness
for survival. The Queen of the Woods, the great earth-goddess, the
eternal female principle venerated by myth throughout the centuries, alone could restore order — but *post mortem*. In *The Anathemata* Jones renominates and celebrates the liturgy as the redemp-
tive order for the living, as an art form. The wine and the bread suffice in that Christ become man blessed the works of man and commanded a "perpetual showing" of the art for His remembrance
and man's salvation.

The bewildered Chorus in Auden's *For the Time Being* asks
plaintively: "How could the Eternal do a temporal act / The In-
finite become a finite fact?"[14] It is a question to which, in a very
real sense, *The Anathemata* proposes a most convincing answer. In
intention and scope Jones's poem is truly epic and might be said to
rival in ambition Milton's attempt to "justify the ways of God to

Men" for an age which urges art to be at the service of the ego, the State, or itself. In Jones's scheme of divine and universal things, "art for art's sake," were he to endorse Wilde's phrase, would reverberate with the utmost seriousness. In the Eucharist is central order, the ordering principle of art, a divinely ordained analogue of Wallace Stevens's jar "upon a hill in Tennessee." To the extent that *The Anathemata* is a made object, embodying the deposits it uncovers and ordering them as new and valid *signa*, it is a success and confirms the theory of its preface. To the extent that Jones's fear that "it may be that the kind of thing I have been trying to make is no longer makeable in the kind of way in which I have tried to make it" (p. 15) is true — that is, that these "fragments of an attempted writing" remain fragments — the poem might be seen to fall short, not yet "anathemata" in all its parts.

CHAPTER 5

The Sleeping Lord

I *Introduction*

J ONES'S last volume of poetry, *The Sleeping Lord: and other fragments*, was published in 1974, the year of his death. Of the nine "fragments" or poems that make up the volume, all had appeared previously except a fragment from "The Book of Balaam's Ass," which had its origins as far back as 1937. The poems had appeared variously in literary magazines from 1955 to 1967, and two, "The Fatigue" and "The Tribune's Visitation," had appeared as separate volumes in limited editions. The works could not possibly be mistaken as having been wrought by any hand other than Jones's, and the concerns they express, the sources they exploit, the imagery, the verse-forms, the annotations, are immediately traceable back to the author of *In Parenthesis*, published some thirty-seven years earlier. Whether or not they "show a sustained music and rhythmic invention finer than anything David Jones had achieved before," as is claimed on the book's jacket, is another question. For Jones and for most of his critics *The Anathemata* was his supreme achievement, and some of these fragments, which Jones once described as "all the pieces I left out of *The Anathemata*,"[1] should be considered as "lesser" works, perhaps, if only in that they are necessary limited in scope by their length.

Their scope, however, is still broad and serious, and the volume does achieve a unity, a cohesiveness, of its own. After the personal, prayerful, and brief "*A,a,a, Domine Deus*" come four poems: "The Wall," "The Dream of Private Clitus," "The Fatigue," and "The Tribune's Visitation," which have as their setting the Mediterranean world, more particularly Rome or Jerusalem, at the time of or surrounding the Crucifixion. "The Tutelar of the Place"

serves to link that group with "The Hunt" and "The Sleeping
Lord," which are set, as it were, in early medieval, Arthurian times
and engage the figure of Arthur as successor to Christ. The fragment from "The Book of Balaam's Ass" with which the volume
concludes is set in the trench world of *In Parenthesis*, but like that
poem and all of Jones's work it again reaches back to the older
orders of Rome and the foundations of empire and Christianity. In
one sense then they contain nothing new in theme; each poem is,
however, "new" in the more important sense (for Jones) in that it
"re-presents" and recalls in a newly made *objet d'art* some valid
signa from the deposits of the past. That was his lifelong concern as
an artist, whether "making" either an epic or a miniature. The
uninitiated reader might well find Jones to be more accessible if he
were to start with this volume; at the same time, Jones makes no
concession to slackness and there can be no denying that the
characteristic difficulties remain. Not one of these poems is slight
or unimportant; they form part of the complex whole that is David
Jones's life work, and while they might be said to be repetitious of
themes often reiterated in *Epoch and Artist* and methods already
exemplified in *In Parenthesis* and *The Anathemata*, each deserves
and rewards individual attention.

II   "A, a, a, Domine Deus"

The first poem of the collection, and one of the earliest in first
draft or conception with its beginnings and abandonment in 1938,
is *"A, a, a, Domine Deus,"* excerpted in the "Art and Sacrament"
essay of 1955 and first published whole in 1966. It is by far the
shortest of Jones's poems, being of but twenty-eight lines; it is the
most personal or confessional, heavily dependent on the pronoun
"I," which is not given any tint of a *persona* beyond the poet himself. In its rhetorical and syntactical simplicity it is quite unlike any
other of Jones's works; it is without annotation and needs none. In
these respects it is decidedly untypical. However, it is distinctly of
David Jones in its admixture of poetry and prose forms; in its imagery, from sources secular and religious, the battlefield and the altar
("I have felt for His Wounds / in nozzles and containers"); and in
the poet's concern to seek out the presence of God in an age of
"dead forms / causation projects from pillar to pylon." Jones's
voice in the poem is that of the artist who, before he knows what to
write, has to enquire, calling into service all the senses, notably the

tactile sense, at his disposal. An image that appears near the end of the poem in that of a lighthouse (typically nautical), which the poet examines to see if the geared wheels which make the light shine forth, if but intermittently, might indeed serve to project the living God. He has asked of the "perfected steel" that it "be my sister" (the familiar search for the female principle), but the critical, judgmental eye and touch of the artist find in the steel and "glassy towers" the "glazed work unrefined and the terrible crystal a stage-paste" (p. 9). That is, there is no workmanship and mere theatrical props pass for the real things that would project or show forth the things of God and man. There are in all manifestations of man the technician no valid *signa* of the presence of Christ or of man the art-making creature; and the poem ends on a tone reminiscent of Hopkins's "terrible sonnets" in its anguished outcry, "*Eia, Domine Deus*." It is the only poem in Jones in which we can discern unmistakably the poet's voice speaking in its own right on its own behalf, but for all that virtue and the virtue of relative simplicity, it is not a mode or voice that is congenial to Jones's real preoccupations as a poet.

III   *"The Wall"*

"The Wall" was written "c. 1952, but using, in part some fragments written c. 1940," and on publication in *Poetry* (Chicago) in 1955 (largely through the good offices and aid of Vernon Watkins) won the Harriet Monroe Memorial Prize. It too is short, but five pages long, and is published without any annotation by Jones. The "wall" of the title is that which both contains and maintains the Roman world, "a megalopolis that wills death." The speaker of the monologue has no name, rank, or serial number, but he has done twenty years of service in "that walk of life" on guard duty. He is not hired or paid to think or to be a poet ("It's not for the likes of you or me to cogitate high policy"), but it is his right, as has been the right of soldiers in any service throughout time, to grumble, to criticize, to raise unanswerable questions. The "you" to whom he addresses his remarks and questions is not identified except as the speaker's "comrade," and the fragment cannot be described literally as a dramatic monologue since there is no internal drama or exchange being enacted or implied. Despite his repeated disclaimer of "we don't know the ins and outs," the unknown soldier has indeed contemplated the why's and wherefore's of his Empire's mili-

tarism — "the robber walls of the world city" (p. 14.), he calls the
boundary he defends — but is unable finally to overcome the habits
instilled in him over twenty years of service. He claims to see
through the war-machine's propaganda, but when the official line
says, in effect, that the Department of War is to be renamed the
Department of Defense, that "the Quirinal Mars turns out to be
no god of war but of armed peace," he invokes memories of past
military exploits and rejoices that he's "helped a lot of Gauls and
gods to die" (p. 14). Jones's old soldier is disgusted that he works
now in defense of "shopkeepers [who] presume to make / the
lupine cry their own":

> Did the empyreal fires
> Hallow the chosen womb
> to tabernacle founders of
> emporia?   (p. 11)

It is no great leap from "founders of emporia" to a middle-class
"nation of shopkeepers" (a phrase attributed to Napoleon at St.
Helena) to later shopping centers and multinational chain stores:
all in service of "Plutus, the gold-getter, and they say that sacred
brat has a future" (p. 14). But the guard concludes, despite the de-
based pecuniary motives for which he is required to serve, that at
least he and his comrade still serve the old god, Mars:

> . . . we shall continue to march and to bear
> in our bodies the marks of the Marcher — by whatever
> name they call him . . .
> we shall continue to march
> round and round the cornucopia:
> that's the new fatigue   (p. 14).

The method, which alludes to legend regarding the founding,
and to history regarding the expansion of, Rome is familiar, as are
the Latin phrases scattered throughout, the free verse form, the
perpetually questioning voice. It is noteworthy that this is pre-
Christian Rome; for Jones's jaded speaker there is as yet no new
god to replace the old, there is only debasement of the old. As with
the boast of Dai Greatcoat in *In Parenthesis*, it is pointless to ask
for "realism" of language; what Jones is doing is taking the liberty, the license, of giving voice to the concerns, otherwise inarticu-

late though not the less real for that, which are part of the consciousness of a low-ranked soldier of that time — and of this.

IV   *"The Dream of Private Clitus"*

The same technique is to hold in "The Dream of Private Clitus,"
in which the speaker of the monologue (it is interrupted but once
for a ten-word question) is a Roman soldier of long service serving
guard-duty on the walls of Jerusalem. Within the monologue
frame, it is the recounting by Private Clitus of a dream he had
dreamed many years earlier while in service in Germany. His "but-
ty" at the time had been one Lugobelinos (Llywelyn in modern
Welsh), a Celt in service of the Empire who, until a "stray" got
him, had "reckoned himself as Ilian and as Urban as the Twins"
(p. 16) — that is, thoroughly "Roman." Clitus now is retelling his
dream (largely in prose, and the piece is almost a short story in
style) to his new companion, one Oenomaus, a Greek recruit of
about one year service. The setting, then, is Roman Jerusalem at a
time preceding the Passion; the principals in the tale are a native
Roman, Greek, and Celt "serving in the same Roman unit to sym-
bolise the heterogeneous nature of the Empire" (p. 15). Jones's
notes to the poem are characteristically diffident and at the same
time illuminating and honest as he justifies his taking of the requisite poetic license. That is,

I do not know whether in fact this could have occurred at that date,
probably not. I chose the name Clitus because to me it felt Roman,
actually it is a Greek name. I may also have got it muddled up in my mind
with Cletus whose name one hears each time one goes to a Mass of the
Roman Rite, though that name too is I believe Greek. But I do not feel
inclined to alter it now   (p. 15).

It is not then the historicity of the occasion that matters; the
poem is centered on a "dream" and the dream-truth, and as Clitus
recounts: "There's no end to the unions these sleep-dreams can
lend to things separate enough in wake-a-day... there's no end to
the possibilities of these dreams" (pp. 18–19). It turns out later, by
the poem's end, that there is in fact at least one thing "that can't be
managed / even in these dreams," and that is the voice of Brasso
Olenius of No. 1 Cohort: "he was up there with us, he's always
been with us, he always will be with us" (p. 21). He is the profes-

sional soldier concerned more with his promotion than any other truths — "we called him Brasso Germanicus." It was Brasso who interrupted the dream of the young legionary in his first year of service, and the sad truth is that one cannot conceive of, either waking or dreaming, a world, an empire, "Dea Roma, Flora Dea / meretrix or world-nutricula" that will not include its Brasso, the cynic, the super-rationalist, the statistician: "There's always a Brasso to shout the odds, a fact-man to knock sideways and fragmentate these dreamed unities and blessed conjugations" (p. 21).

The dream Clitus had been enjoying, before being so rudely interrupted by Brasso, had him and Lugobelinos bivouacked beneath the *Tellus Mater* statue at the entrance to Rome and privileged in the vision to be embraced by the *Tellus Mater*, Earth Mother, herself. It is an anticipation of the death (cf. the Queen of the Woods in *In Parenthesis*) that was indeed to come to Lugobelinos: "when they got him I was next by him in the traverse — and that was no dream" (p. 20). But Jones's chief concern is with the language in which one addresses the tutelary spirits of the earth.

> And now (in my dream-now that is), from his side our
> gestatorial marble, Lugo cried out a name: Modron!
> he cries, and then, — but very low-voiced though:
> Porth-Annwfyn. Some numinous, arcane agnomen, but which
> to my dream cognition was as lucid as moonshine and
> did plainly signify: Gate of Elysium.
>
> Now I know no word of Lugo's lingo, and it was, after
> all *my* dream, not his. Well, Oenomaus, what do you
> make of that one?   (p. 20)

When later Lugo caught his "stray one" (whether in the Roman age or during World War I is not really made explicit and doesn't matter at all) "he cried loud the same cult name, but not the last bit, for he was done before he could utter it."

> So, as I figure it, his Modron and our Matrona are one,
> and his *porth* that shadowy portal beyond which Proserpine
> abides, from fall till crocus-time   (p. 20).

To translate the words is in some way to miss the point entirely. It is a point reiterated in Jones from *In Parenthesis* to *The Anathemata* and given special emphasis in "The Tutelar of the Place."

There is but one Earth Mother of us all; she delights not in Empire, uniformity, but in variety, locality; each must speak to her in his native tongue as did Dai Greatcoat at his death and the mariners praying for divine protection on their first voyage to the shores of Britain — all the Brasso's and Sergeant Quilters of the world notwithstanding. There is in a poem by W. H. Auden a felicitous "misprint" that the poet allowed to stand which reinforces the point Jones is after: Auden first wrote "the poets have names for the sea," but "poets" came out "ports."[2] There's nothing wrong with the first writing, but the principle of local *agnomena* or naming of sea, or god, or underworld, or spirits tutelar is central to an understanding of what David Jones is about.

V   *"The Fatigue"*

In "The Fatigue," first published in 1965 as a specially printed edition "as a token of affection and esteem from friends and admirers" in honor of Jones's seventieth birthday, the major voice is that of a Roman *principalis* ("identified in my mind with a Cockney N.C.O.," Jones notes) to the recruits who are in his charge; the time is the night before the Crucifixion; the setting, Jerusalem. Jones appended a full set of notes for this fragment, not confining himself merely to annotation of historical, linguistic, and referential detail, but also outlining his strategy and intention. As in "The Dream of Private Clitus," he is concerned less with possible falsifying of history in having Celts from Gaul or Britain serving with the Roman troops than the "far more important historical truth: the heterogeneous composition of the forces of a world-imperium" (p. 24).

After a brief scene-setting by dialogue, the poem continues with the voice of the "Sergeant" berating his men: "It's whoresons like you as can't keep those swivel eyes to front one short *vigilia* through as are diriment to our unific and expanding order" (p. 28), and calling for Crixus, "that insubordinate Gallic buddy of yours" (p. 29). For the voices in the poem, of course, the Crucifixion can be said in a sense already to have happened; liturgical or biblical language is laced throughout the speeches of the *principalis*, his superiors back at Rome, and the voice of the composite soldier musing on what the next day will bring. In the literal present of the poem, however, the point being made is that those who will serve at the moment of the Crucifixion will be, unwittingly and without

choice, those selected by the routines of military administrative
necessity for the job. The process begins at headquarters back in
Rome:

> From where an high administration deals in world-
> routine down through the departmental meander
> winding the necessities and accidents
> the ball rolls slowly
> but it rolls
> and on it your name and number   (p. 39).

At the field level, it will be as much a matter of chance; some men
will indeed participate intimately in the imminent earth-shaking
transformation of the world, of the Empire, that quite literally
knows not what it does. The *principalis* / sergeant concludes:

> By your place on a sergeant's roster
> by where you stand in y'r section
> by *when* you fall in
> by if they check you from left or right
> by a chance numbering-off
> by a corporal's whim
> you will furnish
> that Fatigue   (p. 41).

All the men will be required for some related duty — some for
escort, some for the hanging, some for digging, some for guard
duty after the event; in the meantime they are directed in timeless
military fashion to "keep that regulation step," to "complete the
routine" then as now.

There is dramatic irony of course in that the modern reader
knows more than the men or the *principalis* of what is to, or did,
happen; more subtly, there is a double verbal irony, in that the
voices throughout the poem are made to speak the language not
only of twentieth-century noncommissioned officers barking
orders but of post-Christian scholars, poets, priests, and believers.
Such "anachronism" is a time-honored technique or device in
poetry; it defines Browning's "Cleon" and "An Epistle . . . Karshish"; Yeats's play *The Resurrection*, Eliot's "The Journey of the
Magi," Auden's *For the Time Being*, Housman's "The Carpenter's
Son," works dealing with the same period in history, the same
theme, and depending for an understanding not only on the histori-

city of the event but on the reader's perception of the verbal and dramatic irony. Jones carries on the method in "The Tribune's Visitation," set not on so precise date as the Passion, but capable of having occurred at any time during the first three decades *Anno Domini.*

VI   *"The Tribune's Visitation"*

"The Tribune's Visitation" was also published as a separate volume (in 1969), and it deals with the "surprise visitation" of a military tribune to troops at his command, such troops being, again, of "mixed recruitment" for the larger poetic truth. There is a sense in which it is a more "realistic" poem than "The Fatigue"; after the initial scene setting it is a virtual monologue by the visiting tribune, who reveals himself to be so human and vulnerable in spirit to the sacred things of his origins as to undermine the demands of his official position and responsibility. It is a more direct and easily decipherable fragment than much of Jones's other poetry; the situation is clear, the speaker readily identifiable as a human, rather than a literary, voice; and the poem is virtually his monologue. The soldiers who are his audience are clearly delineated, by rank, name, even by serial number (but in twentieth-century English: sergeant, corporal, private, etc.), and they react to his speech, which disturbs their expectations and makes them uncomfortable but captive listeners. The tribune is perhaps the most sympathetically portrayed of all Jones's speakers; this is not the private's grumble or retailing of dreams, not the sergeant's barking of orders, but the Commanding Officer's crucial self-examination, in public.

His audience is made up of soldiers of the poem's present and of the future, Roman soldiers guarding the walls of Empire and British soldiers in the trenches of France, all "men at a specific but recurring moment in *urbs*-time" (p. 50) and all sensitive to the mingled sounds of songs on the hills of ancient Italy and "some high hill-cymanfa" in Wales. The tribune explores intimately what it is one in his position is called upon to render unto Caesar, and speaks first as a "forthright Roman" for Caesar and for Empire:

> The loricas of Caesar's men
> should shine like Caesar
> back and front
> whose thorax shines all ways

                        and to all quarters
                        to the world-ends
            whether he face unstable Britain
                        or the weighty Persians   (p. 48).

Then he has "a word to say to you as men and as a man speaking to
men" (p. 50), and the monologue is poised from that point on between the demands of the military and the personal as the tribune
"uses" the silent, disturbed, perhaps cowed men whom he has sur-
prised to pose what are really his own questions:

These several streams, these local growths, all that belongs to the fields of
Latium, to the Italic fatherland, surely these things, these dear pieties,
should be remembered?   (p. 51)

He answers his own nonquestion in the only way possible or plau-
sible, dismissing the idea that recognition of such "deep things"
would make them "better men, the better soldiers, so the better
friends of Caesar":

                        No, not so
            that pretty notion, too, must go.
                        Only the neurotic
            look to their beginnings   (p. 51).

And Rome's men must learn to "spurn the things of Saturn's Tellus" lest they fall victim to the same kind of soft romanticizing that
characterized Private Clitus's dream.

            Then comes the Tribune's public confession and identification:
            I too could weep
                        for these Saturnian spells
            and for the remembered things.
                        If you are Latins
            so am I   (p. 52).

The men at his command he embraces verbally and in his gestures
as his brothers, and as the poem proceeds the tribune takes on more
of the attributes of priest than officer. He voices sentiments that
are dangerously subversive, enough, he knows, to have him stripped
of office, and the by-now tribune *cum* priest *cum pater familias*

speaks the language of St. Paul in the epistles. Finally, in his performing the act central to Christianity, central in David Jones's poetry, he declares: "See! I break this barrack bread, I drink with you, this issue cup, I salute, with you, these mutilated signa" (p. 58). By the poem's conclusion the word "illusion" to describe the things of the spirit, of the past, has been seen to apply to the apparent "realities" of the situation; this tribune, like the St. Paul whose language he anticipates so faithfully, is perhaps a forerunner of that Roman who was converted on the road to Damascus. He is ready for a light to bring deliverance, and is ripe for conversion not to a wholly new God or wholly new set of "*signa*," but because he perceives that the "ratifying formula, *idem in me*," the brotherhood of sharing bread and water, the military oath of *sacramentum*, testify not to subversion or breakup but to the deepest historical and spiritual continuities.

VII   "*The Tutelar of the Place*"

The poem is published without preface or annotation (save for a brief glossary of Welsh words provided by Vernon Watkins for its first printing in *Poetry* [Chicago] in 1961) and is clear and persuasive. It is, Jones writes, "a companion piece" to "The Tribune's Visitation," but it is not set in the world of the Roman Empire and is not a monologue by a fictitious voice. What it shares with that poem, and enlarges beyond that poem, is the theme of the sanctity of the local place and the local goddess. The poem is both descriptive and didactic; the female tutelary spirit is at once the great Earth Mother, "Tellus of the myriad names," the Virgin Mary, and "Great-Jill-of-the-tump-that-bare-me"; and to approach her and gain her intervention and life-giving intercession we must recognize her as a local habitant, use local language, not "cry by some new fangle . . . name" that is alien to her in her place.

> She that loves place, time, demarcation, hearth, kin,
> enclosure, site, differentiated cult, though she is but
> one mother of us all: one earth brings us all forth,
> one womb receives us all, yet to each she is other
> named of some other . . .   (p. 59).

The first part of the poem is given to enumerating her maternal qualities and concludes with Jones's version of the "teach us to pray" request of the apostles. What follows is not the Lord's but the child's prayer as taught by the poet; conspicuously, it is addressed not to "our Father which art in heaven" but to our Mother, who is on earth, is in fact the earth, our local habitant:

> Say now little children:
> Sweet Jill of our hill hear us
> bring slow bones safe at the lode-ford
> keep lupa's bite without our wattles
> make her bark keep children good
> save us all from dux of far folk
> save us from the men who plan.
> Now sleep on, little children, sleep on now, while
> I tell out the greater suffrages, not yet for young
> heads to understand   (pp. 61–62).

The second half of the poem is then an adult's prayer to the same "Jill," addressed now as "Queen of the differentiated sites ... mother of particular perfections / queen of otherness / mistress of asymmetry / ... mediatrix of all the deposits" (p. 62), and it is a prayer that rings down through the centuries. First it is the cry of the local Celts against the spreading Roman armies and administrators:

> In all times of imperium save us when the
> *mercatores* come save us
> from the guile of the *negotiatores* save us
> / from the *missi*
> from the agents ...
> When they proscribe the diverse uses and impose the
> rootless uniformities, pray for us   (p. 62).

As the prayer proceeds the poem becomes even more specifically Welsh, as the Ram moves through the centuries and becomes not so much Rome as Westminister or the seat of the unified central government; from remote history the prayer comes for protection "in the days of the central economies ... in the bland megalopolitan light" (p. 63). The child's Jill, the *Tellus Mater*, or Earth Mother or Queen, gives way to "Sweet Mair" as the Welsh-Catholic voice of the poet follows his own "instructions" of the first part of the poem and addresses her in her local name (*Mair* is Welsh for Mary):

> ... where the dark outcrop
> >   tells on the hidden seam
> pray for the green valley ...
> Remember the mound-kin, the kith of the *tarren*
> gone from this mountain because of the exorbitance
> of the Ram ... remember them in the rectangular
> tenements, in the houses of the engines that fabricate
> the ingenuities of the Ram ... Mother of Flowers save
> them then where no flower blows   (p. 63).

The reference to the coalseams that have been the material wealth of Wales is evident, as are references to the rows of grimy terrace houses and factories that still scar the coal-mining valleys. It is a far more obvious political statement than Jones allows himself in any other of the poems, yet it is not narrowly political in the sense that it takes sides in, say, whether the coal mines should or should not be nationalized. One gathers that Jones despises equally both kinds of "rootless uniformities," and in one sense the poem is in retreat as it craves the beneficence of "ventricle and refuge both, *hendref* for world-winter, asylum from world-storm" in "Womb of the Lamb the spoiler of the Ram" (p. 64). It is thoroughly Romantic, almost Wordsworthian, in its initial celebration of the simple innocence of the children learning how to pray; it is also thoroughly Christian as it echoes the phrasing of Nicodemus to ask that we may "enter a second time" into the womb. In short it is asking for a rebirth through the protection and intercession of *Mair* or the Virgin Mary that will enable man and child, Jack of the Tump, to survive the "world-storm" in the latter day, "the December of our culture" (p. 64).

Jones is always happiest looking backward, but he looks for signs that will revalidate life today. In the verse fragments there is both a fear of Apocalypse and faint hope for survival; in "The Sleeping Lord" is expressed a muted, rather than sure and certain, hope that the spirit of Arthur will again revivify the Wasted Land. That the next Arthur might come again as *dux bellorum* or the most ruthless technocrat-administrator of them all is not a possibility Jones wants to consider. Jones articulated no system such as Yeat's *A Vision*, and his prayer in "The Tutelar of the Place" is noticeably different in its particular requests than that poet's "A Prayer for My Daughter," But the perceived threat of a cycle of human civilization about to undergo catastrophe is not far different from that expressed in Yeats's "The Second Coming."

VIII   *"The Hunt"*

David Jones writes of "The Hunt" that "this fragment is part of an incomplete attempt based on the native Welsh early medieval prose-tale *Culhwch ac Olwen*, in which the predominant theme becomes the great hunt across the whole of southern Wales of the boar Trwyth by all the war-bands of the Island led by Arthur." Published first in 1965, it was written "c. 1964 incorporating passages written c. 1950 or earlier" (p. 69). Although based on a tale from the *Mabinogion*, the poem deals with only a small fraction of that book, in which the boarhunt is but a small part. Jones's attention is on, first, the gathering of the *arglwyddi*, the noblemen, who pursue the boar Trwyth for sundry reasons: "the lords who ride after deep consideration and the lords whose inveterate habit is to ride the riders who ride from interior compulsion and the riders who fear the narrow glances of the kindred" (p. 66). The prey itself, the rampaging Trwyth, who laid waste much of Ireland, Wales, and Cornwall, does not appear anywhere in the poem, except implicitly as the cause of the action. Jones's chief interest is in the figure of Arthur, at the center of the gathering, at the center of the poem. He is lord among lords, at the height of his regal stature and at the height of personal strength and vigor. But he shows his wounds; he shows the strain of leadership. He is:

> . . . the diademed leader
> who directs the toil
> whose face is furrowed
> with the weight of the enterprise
> the lord of the conspicuous scars whose visage
> is fouled with the hog-spittle whose cheeks are fretted
> with the grime of the hunt-toil   (p. 67).

The identification of Arthur with Christ is deliberate and pervasive throughout, from his "twisted diadem," the "countless points of his wounds," and his "scarred feet"; and the fragment breaks beyond local Welsh adventure, beyond retailing of myth, and becomes an account of the massing of an earthbound heavenly host. Unlike the lords previously mentioned who ride for various earthbound reasons, Arthur rides "for the healing of the woods / and because of the hog,"

> And if through the trellis of green

> and between the rents of the needle-work
> the whiteness of his body shone
> so did his dark wounds glisten   (p. 68).

In the last lines the identification of this hunt with Christ's crucifixion and, by implication, His harrowing of Hell, is made explicit:

> because this was the Day
> of the Passion of the Men of Britain
> when they hunted the Hog
> life for life   (p. 69).

A magnificent description and characterization of Jones's Arthur, it is but a brief fragment detailing a pause in the actual hunt;
one cannot but feel regret that Jones was unable to or chose not to
develop the work further.

IX *"The Sleeping Lord"*

This fragment, more so than any of the others, is of a piece with
The Anathemata. The central action is that of the Priest of Arthur's household celebrating a Requiem Mass, in which he invokes
the post-Christian litany and rollcall of heroes of the island, both
mythic and historic. Arthur, like Llywelyn, the last Welsh "Prince
of Wales," who was killed in 1282, is dead — but not really, for he
but slumbers. The "Director of Toil" has earned his rest; the hun-
ter of the Boar Trwyth detailed in "The Hunt" sleeps deeply but also fitfully, uncertain, like his "drowsing mate" (presumably
Llywelyn), whether the noises that disturb his slumber are the real
call or but the wind. The poem has a modern political significance
in that it looks consciously at the land of Wales ancient and
modern; it is ancient in that it invokes the complex deposits of
Christian and Welsh pagan mythology. There is no single voice or
focus in the poem; its principals are Arthur's candlebearer, his
footholder, and his priest of the household, and the only moments
of action are those in which the candlebearer, without liturgical authority but quite spontaneously, responds to the priest's whispered
"Requiem aeternam dona eis, Domine" in a "high clear and distinct voice, the response: *ET LUX PERPETUA LUCEAT EIS"*
(p. 87). Much of the poem, like *The Anathemata*, is made up of

questions, largely rhetorical, that seek to establish not the local site
of Arthur's grave, but to establish his presence throughout the land
and speculate on whether or not he will come again:

> ... are the hills his couch
> or is he the couchant hills?
> Are the slumbering valleys
> him in slumber
> are the still undulations
> the still limbs of him sleeping ...?
> Does the land wait the sleeping lord
> or is the wasted land
> that very lord who sleeps?   (p. 96)

The poem is *The Anathemata* in miniature, in that the central act
performed is the Mass, the recalling, which occasion Jones uses to
invoke time and "deposits" from the pre-Cambrian Ice Age to the
present. It is different to the degree that the body recalled or celebrated is more specifically that of Arthur than Christ, though the
coidentity of the two is never in doubt. For example: Arthur's footholder performs the same office as did "Mair Modlen" (Mary
Magdalene) in caring for "the eternally pierced feet / of the Shep-
herd of Greekland / the Heofon-Cyning / born of Y Forwyn
Fair" (p. 73). Passages of intensely thickened and tangled mythic
recalling (e.g., "coursing through the bleaker house of The-Man-
that-Pours-the-Water-Out, careens on his fixed and predetermined
cursus, with the axle tree of his essedum upward steeved ...") are
all in the service of the central political question (as distinct from
the central commemorative act of the Mass) that Jones states very
explicitly indeed.

> How? Why?
> It is because of the long, long
> and continuing power-struggle
> for the fair lands of Britain
> and the ebb & flow of the devastation-
> / waves of the war-bands
> for no provinces of the West
> were longer contested than these provinces
> nor is the end yet
> for that tide rises higher
> nor can it now be stayed   (p. 80).

The ministering priest's "silent, brief and momentary recalling" to his Lord Arthur does issue then in the hope, obliquely held, that there shall be an awakening, that the composite Cronos/ Christ/Arthur/Owain /Llywelyn figure will indeed rise again and restore the wasted land.

Unlike the Palestinian or Roman fragments, this poem had its origins and writing from "November 1966 to March 1967" (p. 96), and is clearly post-*Anathemata* in its concept and construction. Even in its last appearance as title poem of the volume, it was considered by Jones as "subject to revision" and incomplete. Jones noted too that "it chances to be a piece that is essentially for the ear rather than the eye" (p. 70), and provided a thorough gloss for the translation and pronunciation of the Welsh words. It is a point worth making about all of Jones's poetry; nothing less than a slow, deliberative, and voiced reading will suffice — and that, more than once; to hear Jones's own recordings of his work is to gain a far richer appreciation of the varieties and intricacies of sound and stress that so inform the meaning.

X   *From "The Book of Balaam's Ass"*

The story of Balaam's ass is told in the Old Testament Book of Numbers, and is concerned with the summoning of Balaam by Balak, the leader of Moab, to recruit him, as it were, to help curse and smite the Israelites. Balaam's ass recognizes the Angel of the Lord blocking his master's way; Balaam does not, and smites his ass three times, despite the voiced pleas of the beast to acknowledge the long and faithful service it has rendered him. Balaam then recognizes the intervention of the Lord and proceeds not to fulfill the request of Balak, but to use the occasion to bless, rather than curse, the Chosen People. The relevance of the biblical story to this fragment (the setting is the 1914–1918 War and the piece is very definitely one with *In Parenthesis*) is not immediately apparent, except only that Jones's narrator is made to speak strange "truths." The voice, except for one brief interlude of *Anathemata*-like poetic elaboration, is decidely prosy, sometimes Cockney, and celebrates, if that is the word, not only the fallen but more importantly those who escaped: Private Lucifer, Private Shenkin, and Private Austin — "But for all the rest there was no help on that open plain" (p. 111). It is as close as Jones comes anywhere to narrative plain-style, though the poet invokes the by-now-familiar rollcall from the past, including here his own characters, Clitus (from "The Dream

of Private Clitus") and Crixus (from "The Fatigue"). It echoes
"The Tutelar of the Place" in that the wounded and dying cry out
in their native language "according to what breasts had fed them"
(p. 110), but in one major and interesting respect this fragment is
unique in Jones's writing.

To recount its "narrative" is both to see that which is typical in
Jones and that which, at first glance, might seem to be most open
to serious quarrel or objection. It is also to see in a very direct way
Jones raising, in a manner that is intensely self-critical, questions of
the value system he honors elsewhere and in this poem. The narrative "I" (Balaam's ass?) can be likened to an old soldier telling an
account of his service at the front; he identifies himself with "poor
boring old Spud [Bullen], the tedious old sweat" who had bored
him and his companions with accounts of service in exotic places;
and further with one "Emeritus Nodens of the 2nd Adjutrix who
regaled them with tales of the elusive Pict" (p. 98) many centuries
earlier. His audience is made up of those who are "regular at the
rails, smilers at flag-day corners, blameless, not extortionate,
superior to party, not loving their own selves, bird-watchers and in-
ventors of humane bull-slaying, temperate, fair-spoken, apprecia-
tive" (p. 97) — in short, his civilian reader. But that group is to include Hector from *The Iliad*, "whose arse they couldn't see for dust
at the circuit of the wall" and Shakespeare's Pistol from *Henry V*,
whom he castigates: "Gee! I do like a bloody lie turned gallantly
romantical, fantastical, glossed by the old gang from the foundations of the world" (p. 99). As the speaker continues to upbraid
Pistol: "Press every allusion into your Ambrosian racket, ransack
the sacred canon and have by heart the sweet Tudor magician,
gather your sanctions and weave your allegories, roseate your
lenses, serve up the bitter dregs in silver-gilt, bless it before and
behind and swamp it with baptismal and continual dew"
(pp. 99–100), the reader just might see an outspoken indictment of
Jones's own methods.

The poem goes on to hold rollcall of the fallen in battle, finding
for each no availing sanctuary on the bare plain: "Lieutenant Fairy
. . . can take thought if he likes from now till zero, he won't add a
cubit of cover for himself nor all his franks" (p. 100); not for "sig-
naller Balin and his incompatible messmate linesman Balan"
(p. 101); not for "three poor men / bible punchers / whose souls
are with Jesus" (p. 103); not for the men of Ireland who had three
times earlier assaulted this mill. The reader might well ask along

with Jones: "And what of His sure mercies that He swore in the ancient days?" (p. 104). "The foxes have holes" but the soldiers on all sides have "Sweet Fanny Adams" (or F. A.). No matter to whom the fallen cry — "some creature of their own kind by name" or "On God and Father of Heaven ... God the Word ... the Lamb ... the Son of Man ... the son of Mary" or on the Virgin herself or on "Abraham's God ... on the unknown God.... On all the devices of the peoples, on all annointed stones, on fertile goddesses" — in short, all the tutelary gods that Jones's poetry has celebrated — there is no salvation for the living. Only three escape this "diversion" at the mill; and if one sees Jones singling these out and celebrating them, is it to put to nought, when it comes to the living test rather than poetry, the efficacy of his whole ethic, his whole vision of man in his relation to God and history?

Taken literally, at face value, the narrative voice would appear to destroy everything Jones's poetry holds dear. But irony attends the whole gesture, as is made immediately clear in the narrator's recounting of the survivors and the putative reasons for their survival. Private Lucifer is invulnerable because he was "possessed of agility, subtlety and lightness ... [he] stood upright under his fire the most beautifullest of men laughing like anything" and was, in the eyes of the Germans, "but an Annointed Cherub" (pp. 105–106). Private Shenkin survived because "he was the least surefooted of men, and the most ungainly and the most easily confused of any man of the Island of Britain" (p. 106). He chances to stumble into a shallow crater, a "burrow of salvation," and when he can finally stand no longer to listen to the wounded praying to the various deities, leaps his way back to the security of the rear lines. Private Austin was invulnerable "by reason of the suffrages of his mother who served God hidden in a suburb ... because she was believed to be appointed mediatrix there" (p. 110). The irony attending Jones's treatment of these survivors is by now evident; he surely does not agree, as "was urged by some," that "Mrs. Austin conditioned and made acceptable in some round-about way the tomfoolery of the G.O.C. in C." (p. 111).

One message or truth, then, is told: those who survive do so by the merest chance; no explanation (at least none from this narrator's mouth) can possibly be taken seriously. That the deaths and/or survivals occur as "accidents" or at random is, however, no departure itself in Jones's works; it is evident in Part 7 of *In Parenthesis*, and is touched on in the "chance" assignments for duty

at the Crucifixion in "The Fatigue." So while the narrative voice is
to be taken ironically, it is not a simple matter of merely reversing
his apparent meaning. Not easily explainable, especially to those
who complain of the apparent ambiguity of Jones's antiwar stance,
is the perception that there is no efficacy or redemption for the living, not in the bosom of Arthur or of Christ or of the Queen of the
Woods, all of whom minister posthumously.

Jones's prefatory note is helpful in that he says "parts of it were
a harking back to conversations of the immediately post 1914-1918
period and to the later phases of the conflict itself" (p. 97); and
when he notes further that the pages of this fragment "were chosen
as seeming to afford a link of sorts" between *In Parenthesis* and *The
Anathemata*, it must be seen, in retrospect, that "Balaam's Ass"
poses very directly, even blatantly, the problem which was to
occupy Jones throughout his adult life. Balaam's ass does indeed
speak with "forked tongue," as it were; much as Jones would like
to beat his narrator and escape his hindrance, the beast stands in
the way and will not let his master proceed without listening and
heeding. As the last piece in *The Sleeping Lord* volume, it serves
then to send us back to the conflict of the 1914-1918 War and the
beginnings of conflict in David Jones's work in reconciling the
things of God and man.

XI   *Other Poems*

There remain two fragments not collected in *The Sleeping Lord*
volume: "The Kensington Mass" and "The Narrows." "The Kensington Mass" was published first in *Agenda* (Autumn-Winter
1973/4) and as a separate volume in 1975. The work had been first
drafted "c. 1940 and then subsequently lost," and is a poem on
which Jones continued to work until his death. The single-volume
edition is supplemented by draft pages of the manuscript that form
a continuation of the poem as first printed, pieced together by René
Hague. "I imagine," Hague wrote, "that each stage would have
the same sort of pictorial content as this — the cock crowing, Peter,
the unloading, the suggestion of Hellenization, the doctors of the
law, Absalom, the bulk of the cross: and, as in *The Anathemata*,
the images could have come from the round earth's imagined corners."[3] The poem is dedicated "in affectionate recalling" of Father
John O'Connor, who had received Jones into the Church in 1921,
and commences with a detailed observation of an Irish priest celebrating the Mass. From that present it moves back to the night

before the Crucifixion, to the Church's first priest, Peter, and the crowing of the cock that signaled both the fateful dawn and Peter's betrayal of his Lord. Jones links that cock crow with *The Song of Roland* and "the echoing blast / from Roncesvalles," connecting his favorite and familiar concerns of the Mass and Man at War in centuries and battles yet to come. Herod too was up early that morning, and there is ironic contrst between his desire, as relief from the burden of affairs of state, "to follow the chase and take whatever fortune the numina of the groves may grant us," and the kind of pursuit that Jones detailed in "The Hunt" and the figure of Arthur.

The title of "The Narrows," written "c. 1941 and 1973," refers to the English Channel, and the speaker of this pre-Christian Roman monologue is a sentry addressing his comrade Porrex, speculating on the further expansion of the Empire to Britain. Again, dramatic and verbal irony informs the whole poem; the speaker is jaded:

> No end to these wars no end, no end
> at all. No end to the world-enrolments
> that extend the war-shape, to police the
> extending *limes*, that's a certainty.[4]

He describes what he knows of the geography of the place (cf. "Middle-Sea and Lear Sea" in *The Anathemata*) and of the pallid hue of its inhabitants:

> All, all, the total sum of all
> even the very baritus
> of blond, great-limbed, berserk savages
> of the dense Hercynian dark arbor-lands
> is ours now for barrack liturgy
> to keep our peckers up when on West Front
> we mingle the blood built of
> the destined commerce of
> Ilia and the Strider.

Troy, Rome, Cockney slang, allusion to the Western front inform this poem, as does allusion to *Y Gododdin* in the line "All our swords / ring in the heads of mothers" (see *In Parenthesis*), and there is familiar irony (and recollection of Private Clitus's dream) in this pre-Christian fragment:

> So long, Porrex, we'd best not long

be found together twice in one *vigilia*, or
they'll suppose we tell together
the beads of Comrade Spartacus.

XII *Conclusion*

It is very difficult with David Jones to speak of sequential "progress" or "development" in his work, more difficult by far than to
cite or document such movement in Eliot, Yeats, or Auden, to con-
fine examples to poets of the twentieth century. For a start, Jones
was past forty when his first written work was published, and he
was by that time a mature artist, thinker, Catholic, man. Clearly
there was a major step forward in *The Anathemata* (1952), but the
fragments of *The Sleeping Lord* volume, variously dated from 1937
to the time of his death in 1974, do not submit to chronological dis-
covery or ordering. The poems published in the twenty post-*Anathemata* years represent less an advance of theme or perspective than
a backing and filling in of detail; each fragment has its place in the
tapestry that is Jones's life-work. In one sense, having once learned
how to read David Jones an impatient reader might tire of the method and repetition of theme. However, the poetry is in the detail,
often surprising, always precise in its concrete sign and evocation.
The best of these fragments — "The Tutelar of the Place," "The
Tribune's Visitation," "The Hunt" (happily one each from the
mythic, Roman, and Arthurian groups) — succeed in that precision
of frame, action, language, and perspective; it is not just that they
are shorter or simpler than the epics. By way of comparison: a
reader might well be advised to begin his appreciation of Browning
with the monologues of Andrea del Sarto, Cleon, and Fra Lippo
Lippi before engaging the complex integrity of *The Ring and the
Book*. So it is with David Jones that the fragments of *The Sleeping
Lord* point to, open up, and provide an access to *The Anathemata*.

CHAPTER 6

The Modern Context

I *Introduction*

I N his "Note of Introduction" to *In Parenthesis*, T. S. Eliot predicted that when the work was "widely enough known — as it
will be in time — it will no doubt undergo the same sort of detective
analysis and exegesis as the later work of James Joyce and the *Cantos* of Ezra Pound" (p. vii). The prediction has come true, at least
in part, and not only of *In Parenthesis*, and in the last decade a
number of writers (see the Selected Bibliography) have turned their
attention to exploring the themes and further analyzing and anno-
tating the texts of Jones's poetry. There is no "Jones industry" that
would rival that of Joyce, Pound, Dylan Thomas, or Eliot himself, but it would be far from accurate to say that Jones has been ignored or slighted. The context in which he has most consistently
been examined, both for admiration and some criticism, is among
the poets and autobiographers of the 1914–1918 War; i.e., as a
"war poet." He has been attended to also in three other contexts:
as a Welshman, a Roman Catholic, a "modernist," and the better
to assess his place in the world of twentieth-century poetry I shall
discuss him not only among the war poets but in the traditions of
Welsh, or Anglo-Welsh, poets of this century (Dylan Thomas,
R. S. Thomas, and Vernon Watkins), and finally in the company
of Hopkins, Pound, Eliot, and Joyce. The distinctions inevitably
become blurred in practice, of course; no poet or group of poets of
any consequence can be so easily confined, but it is a mark of
Jones's achievement that he can be, indeed must be, reckoned with
on such apparently divergent fronts.

II *Poets of the 1914–1918 War*

"Oh What a Literary War" is the title of one chapter in a recent
book on the subject,[1] and merely to list the names of those poets
who participated in the 1914–1918 War is to hold a rollcall of some
of the most familiar household names in twentieth-century poetry:
Wilfred Owen, John Masefield, Siegfried Sassoon, Rupert Brooke,
Robert Graves; only slightly less familiar perhaps are Ford Madox
Ford, Edmund Blunden, Herbert Read, Charles Sorley, Julian
Grenfell, Edward Thomas, and Isaac Rosenberg. These are, I say,
names familiar enough to readers of modern poetry; at the same
time the list does not include the names of the certified literary
"greats" of the century. Which is not to say that the great ones
shirked their duty, merely to note that for reasons of age, health,
nationality, sex, or passionate revulsion to it, W. B. Yeats, Thomas
Hardy, T. S. Eliot, Ezra Pound, James Joyce, Rudyard Kipling,
D. H. Lawrence, Joseph Conrad, E. M. Forster, Virginia Woolf
were not active participants in the fury and mire of the battlefields
on the continent. To quote T. S. Eliot again: "David Jones is a representative of the same literary generation as Joyce and Pound and
myself. . . . The lives of all of us were altered by that War, but
David Jones is the only one to have fought in it" (p. viii). And it is
of course a moot question, endlessly capable of argument, whether
or not six of the young poets listed above who died in the war
(Brooke, Owen, Sorley, Grenfell, Rosenberg, Edward Thomas)
would, had they lived, eventually have been numbered among the
great.

"In reading the poetry of World War I we . . . see a body of verse
limited to a rather narrow range of personal experience, subjective
and impressionistic in mode, marked by emotional excess, and
motivated by disillusionment, anger, or pity";[2] the critic is John H.
Johnston, who sees Jones alone among the war poets as one given
to "remythologizing" in the language and form of traditional epic
poetry rather than given over wholly to personal reminiscence and
the lyric mode. If *In Parenthesis* is epic, however, it is epic with one
major difference: it has no hero. It has heroic echoes, heroic language, heroic motifs; Jones writes of his comrades that "it was
curious to know them harnessed together, and together caught in
the toils of 'good order and military discipline'; to see them shape
together to the remains of an antique regimental tradition" (p. x)
in the service of their king and his generals. (Jones's first title for
the manuscript was *In Harness on the Right*.)[3] In this century of the

common man the war destroyed daily tens of thousands, and over its four-year course hundreds of thousands, of volunteer and impressed fighting men and commissioned officers, and these are finally its heroes. Heroes, yes, but victims first, and it is as the latter that Jones celebrates them — not, I hasten to add, in the sense that the Prufrockian self-worrying and self-pitying neurotic considers himself as a victim, but in the tradition of Hector, Christ, Arthur, Roland, and Oliver — sacrificers all.

In his preface to *In Parenthesis* Jones quotes approvingly the judgment that if "it is the conservatism and loyalty to lost causes of Western Britain that has given our national tradition its distinctive character, then perhaps the middle ages were not so far wrong in choosing Arthur, rather than Alfred or Edmund or Harold, as the central figure of the national heroic legend" (p. xiii). It is characteristic in Jones, perhaps characteristic of the Welsh consciousness or personality, and evidently characteristic of the body of war poetry from 1914-1918 that it is obsessed with defeat, indeed celebrates it. Rupert Brooke and Julian Grenfell notwithstanding — they died young — there is no war poetry in which a sense of satisfaction is taken in the triumph of a particular battle or in the hope of the eventual victory of the Allies over the Germans. With Jones particularly the celebration of defeat begins with, say, the *felix culpa* of Adam; the destruction of Hector and Troy; the evident defeat of Christ's mission, as some would have had Him, to be an earthly King of the Jews; the slaughter of the Welsh fighting men at Catraeth; the noble deaths of Roland and Oliver at Roncesvalles; the fall of Arthur and his kingdom on earth at Camlann; the killing and beheading of Llywelyn the Great in 1282; and the doomed assault at Mametz Wood by the Royal Welch regiment. The apparent victory of Henry Tudor at Bosworth Field in 1485 is not, cannot be, a cause for Welsh celebration since it was his son, Henry VIII, who in the Acts of Union of 1536 and 1542 forbade the use of Welsh in the law and administration of Wales and hence helped make Wales a cultural wasteland. From the Welsh view, such "victories" carried within them the seeds of their own defeat. And such kinds of historical irony — from the Fall arises a greater good — inform all looking backward. But it is not exclusively of David Jones or of Welsh sensibility; it is of Tennyson very directly, for no other poet of the nineteenth century was so resolute a celebrator of losers as the poet of *Maud*, "Locksley Hall," "The Charge of the Light Brigade," and, of course, *The Idylls of the King*. Ironically, too, as has been noted by Paul Fussell, it was Tennyson and William Morris who in their time did a lot to precondition the attitudes of those who would indeed go to the front; they went quite unprepared for the realities of mechanized warfare and could indeed still think of it in Romantic terms. Fussell sets out a "table of equivalents" of feudal language and its modern counterparts; for example, a friend is a "comrade"; a horse is a "charger" or "steed"; a soldier is "a warrior"; and dead bodies are "ashes" or "dust." The blood of young men is, in the elevated rhetoric of Rupert Brooke, "the red/ Sweet wine of youth."[4]

Given that kind of model, the wonder is that the war poets so quickly learned to put aside soft music and maundering sentiment; their characteristic diction is not Romantic-feudal. It is at another extreme. brutally honest and unflinching in describing blood as blood and war as hell. If there is to be an objection, say, to Graves's "Dead Boche," it is to be made not on the grounds that it flinches from describing the real thing, but that the vision offered is nothing that a particularly gruesome photograph could not do as well, or better. That is, it is documentary, an object lesson, a "certain cure for lust of blood":

> . . . he scowled and stunk
>   With clothes and face a sodden green,
> Big-bellied, spectacled, crop-haired,
> Dribbling black blood from nose and beard.[5]

Siegfried Sassoon wrote that "David" (Robert Graves) was "more easily shocked than I was, he had . . . a first rate nose for anything nasty";[6] Graves in turn said of Sassoon (known as "Mad Jack") that he was a "fire-eater" on the lines: "the number of Germans whom I killed or caused to be killed could hardly be compared with his wholesale slaughter."[7] Graves's lines do indeed evoke revulsion in horror from the visual image; they are intended so to do. Compare too Wilfred Owen's lines in *"Dulce et Decorum Est"*:

> If in some smothering dreams you too could pace
> Behind the wagon that we flung him in,
> And watch the white eyes writhing in his face,
> His hanging face, like a devil's sick of sin;
> If you could hear, at every jolt, the blood
> Come gargling from the froth-corrupted lungs,
> Obscene as cancer, bitter as the cud
> Of vile, incurable sores on innocent tongues. . . .

The language is straining to describe the hitherto undescribed, and the truly horrific so pictured, there is but one "interpretation" left for Owen to make; and he makes it with reference to a heroic model from the past: "If" we could have seen, or if we can now see with eyes newly opened, then

> My friend, you would not tell with such high zest
> To children ardent for some desperate glory,
> The old Lie: *Dulce et decorum est*
> *Pro patria mori.*[8]

Owen is at his maximum extension of language first to shock the senses and then to double the impact by applying savage irony, to which there simply can be no rebuttal. The language of the heroic, of the "classic" model is, it would seem, wrecked for all time, destroyed by the onslaught of Owen's irony; and the question remains whether Jones's attempt to redeem it is even possible.

Jones too is capable of irony:

> you mustn't spill the precious fragments, for perhaps
> these raw bones live.
>   They can cover him again with skin — in their candid
> coats, in their clinical shrines and parade the miraculi.
>   (*IP*, p. 175)

The immediate subject is the imagined treatment of the wounded after the war, but Jones is not dwelling on a gruesome sight and then interpreting it. In a sense he is not "looking" at it at all, but interpreting it immediately, "at sight," by reference to the ministrations of Mary, brother of Lazarus, and the Book of Ezekiel.

Another example, more explicit:

> The blinded one with the artificial guts — his morbid
> neurosis retards the treatment, otherwise he's
> bonza — and will learn a handicraft   (*IP*, p. 176).

No piling on of adjectives would make any stronger the disgust that informs the ironic projection. In the same way, no detailed morbid or horrified description of the corpse would enhance this:

> No one to care there for Aneirin Lewis spilled there
> who worshipped his ancestors like a Chink
> who sleeps in Arthur's lap . . .   (*IP*, p. 155).

"Spilled" and the repetition of "there" as representing the gap
that yawns between those waiting and those already dead says it all;
it is, in a sense, a poetry of "decorum" or restraint, and the irony
that attends the mythic invocation in the lines soon following is
unmistakable:

> Properly organised chemists can let make more riving
> power than ever Twrch Trwyth;
> more blistered he is than painted Troy Towers
> and unwholer, limb from limb, than any of them fallen at
> Catraeth ...   (*IP*, p. 155).

In a word, this war is worse by far than anything one reads about
in "*Culwch ac Olwen*," Homer, or *Y Gododdin*. It is not a mark
either of insensitivity or of flinching; far less is it an attempt to ennoble the slaughter by reference to a mythic past. It is not self-
indulgent language at all; not descriptive or ornamental but tellingly accurate in its account of the present and economical and precise in its evocation of mythic counter-parts. It asks not that we
dwell on the horror of the spectacle before us either for ghoulish
reasons or to evoke cries of "Shame" or "Pity," but forces us to
see the historical continuity of sacrifice. It is not the war recollected
in tranquility, it is the war in all its faces and traces condensed, dis-
tilled, into the moment — concentrated in the present but reaching
beyond it. The "difficulty" in Jones lies not so much in that modern readers might not recognize the allusions, but in the compres-
sion. It is a form given to "re-presenting" the real in immediate
juxtaposition to the past to evoke an unmistakable response
through the unadorned accuracy of its language, both present and,
to use a grammatical term, "present perfect."
    Jones was capable neither of the horrified picturings of Graves
and Owen in the passages cited, nor of the measured prose autobiography, tinged throughout with irony, of Graves, Edmund
Blunden, and Sassoon. To look here just at their titles is to perceive
the kind of distance that those writers were able to manage, albeit
some years after the war: *Goodbye to All That* (1929); *Undertones
of War* (1929); *Memoirs of a Fox-Hunting Man* (1928); and *Memoirs of an Infantry Officer* (1930) — each in its way evokes an
appreciation of the irony that is to be found in the works themselves. Graves, shattered physically and psychically as he undoubt-
edly was, nonetheless seems to have completed his therapy with the
writing of his autobiography to 1928. The title is curt, controlled,

dismissive, "outer." (Compare, for example, Hemingway's *A Farewell to Arms* — there is a literary title, while Graves's is deliberately low-grade and idiomatic.) "That" is the demonstrative pronoun indicating what is outside oneself, outside the instant, distant from the present. For Graves, of course, "that" refers not just to his service in the war but to a whole way of life — upbringing and childhood, schooling at Charterhouse and Oxford, a short-lived career as country shop-keeper, husband to Nancy Nicholson, and professor in Egypt. As he noted in 1957:

I partly wrote, partly dictated, this book twenty-eight years ago during a complicated domestic crisis, and with very little time for revision. It was my bitter leave-taking of England. . . . [9]

Graves looking backward is able to find a number of "caricature scenes" featuring himself — one true mark of a sound mind. Jones's work, by contrast, is rarely marked by humor, certainly not sustained humor. There is little evidence in Graves's later work — literally dozens of writings of poetry, novels, criticism — of any lingering, acute phobia or delayed horror. For David Jones, however, the later breakdowns, the painfully slow, inhibited, extremely diffident, and on balance meager output of literary work, of "fragments of fragments," attest to the lifelong effects of acute trauma. A writer does not erase a "parenthesis"; it forces itself into the text; it is not a footnote or marginal comment to be dismissed or quickly glossed; it is part of the life, its texture, its manner. To make the same point a little more dramatically one need only compare Jones's "The Tutelar of the Place" with Graves's *The White Goddess*, or Jones's Roman fragments with Graves's *I, Claudius*.

It is not finally a matter, in this context, of making judgments of relative worth. David Jones had to labor harder and longer than any other writer of the Great War to present to his Muse a volume "FOR MY FRIENDS IN MIND OF ALL COMMON & HIDDEN MEN AND OF THE SECRET PRINCES," and for all his antiquarian loves he did it in the language of his century. No imitation of the hexameters of Homer and Virgil, or of the heroic couplets of Pope, the onrushing anapests of Byron in *The Destruction of Sennacherib*, nor yet of Wordsworthian or Tennysonian blank verse. His "free" verse has its echoes of and connection with these and other "traditions" — in Malory, early Welsh poetry, Hopkins, the Bible — but it is not that of the Celtic twilight or soft Georgianism. It is of the sinewy strains of twentieth-century poetry at its most demanding and resourceful, not sentimental but tough-minded as befit the occasion, in *In Parenthesis*, of the war in which he was an acutely observant participant.

III   *The Welsh Context*

The term "Anglo-Welsh" has come to designate — not without some heated objection — the work of Welsh poets writing in English, which is in fact the only language of approximately three-quarters of the citizens resident in Wales. It is not a wholly satisfactory term, partly because it immediately gives rise to further questions and narrow subdivisions. There is the question of national "purity," as it were. David Jones, for example, was Welsh only on his father's side; further, he lived virtually his whole life absent from Wales, except for occasional visits and short stays. Yet his poetry is laced throughout with words from the Welsh language, and his lifelong concern for Wales and Welsh literature as subsumed under his larger lifetime quest for the true "Matter of Britain" leaves no question as to his loyalty. One critic claims that David Jones "has been taken in by his Welshness" and goes on to quote Kingsley Amis on the "Welsh cult . . . 'wild valley babblers, woaded with pit dirt and sheep shit, thinking in Welsh the whole time and obsessed by terrible beauty, etc.' " Coffey continues: "More or less as the British starve the Irish, or turn the artillery on Dublin or send in the Tans, they produce literary critics, who exclaim, 'The Celt, how beautiful his soul!' "[10] There is, however, no need to have recourse to any fatuous sentimentality to explain Jones's preoccupation with his "Welshness" or to appreciate the high seriousness of his intention and achievement.

Anglo-Welsh poetry, so designated, is strictly a phenomenon of the twentieth century, and it is to stretch what the term can include beyond any reasonable bounds to invoke it to include the work of Vaughan and Herbert, poetic divines of the seventeenth century. By contrast, unhyphenated Welsh poetry from premedieval times to the present, is not only certifiably ancient but vigorous and alive despite the dwindling numbers of Welsh speakers. Sir H. Idris Bell can speak quite properly and with authority of a renaissance in Welsh letters in the twentieth century because there is a thousand-year history of Welsh literature against which he can measure the modern achievement.[11] But it would be quite inaccurate to use the word "renaissance" to account for what has been happening in Anglo-Welsh poetry since, say, the 1930s; rather the achievement should be described as an initial flowering.

IV   *Dylan Thomas*

The best-known by far of modern Anglo-Welsh poets is, of course, Dylan Thomas, who spoke no Welsh and carried on throughout his foreshortened life a love-hate relationship with the land of his fathers — "and my fathers can keep it."[12] The biographical connections between Jones and Dylan Thomas are slight. They met but two or three times; Jones said of Thomas that he was "a great artist" and expressed his admiration for *Under Milk Wood*,[13] and Thomas performed the part of Dai Greatcoat in a broadcast of *In Parenthesis* and read some of Jones's poetry on one of his reading tours in the United States. In temperament and behavior the men could not have been farther apart, though Thomas was as dedicated to his "craft and sullen art" as was Jones to his vision. Whereas for David Jones the meaning and worth of Wales was to be found in antiquity, in the Welsh mythic, literary, and legendary "deposits" of the British island, for Dylan Thomas it was usually pursued no further than the world of "A Child's Christmas in Wales" and "Fern Hill," works of nostalgia for a lost world of innocence and childhood. There is, however, no denying the importance of Wales as the site of such yearnings, and it is no accident that Wales is at the center, in the only closed couplet, of the "Author's Prologue" to Thomas's *Collected Poems*:

> ... Look:
> I build my bellowing ark
> To the best of my love
> As the flood begins,
> Out of the fountainhead
> Of fear, rage red, manalive,
> Molten and mountainous to stream
> Over the wound asleep
> Sheep white hollow farms
> To Wales in my arms.[14]

There is, however, nothing in Jones so determinedly personal and sexual; and in Thomas's short stories in which he explores, in the occult and symbolic folkways of Welsh life, those darker aspect

of the Welsh psyche that so haunted another Welsh writer, Caradoc
Evans, he is in areas quite alien to David Jones. Where the two
poets might be seen to come together is in their debt to Hopkins
and their passion for reinvigorating the language — coining words,
compounding them, inverting them, punning on them. Thomas
was by far the more given to this kind of invention; Jones was more
concerned with "roots" and reclaiming words long forgotten. For
Thomas, however, language was ever in service of the lyric "I";
Jones strained outward to the epic. In the Welsh tradition, the forerunner of Thomas might be seen in the medieval poet Dafydd ap
Gwilym; for David Jones the bards of the *Mabinogion* and *Y
Gododdin* were the truly ancient and life-giving springs.

V   *Vernon Watkins*

An intimate friend of both Dylan Thomas and David Jones was
Vernon Watkins, who wrote of Jones:

> The best are older: with the unrest time brings,
> No absolute remains to bind them fast.
> One scrawls on rock the names of hallowed things,
> Letter and hieroglyphs that yet shall last
> When darkness measures with a martyr's eye
> The glories shed by life's unchanging tree.[15]

The recent publication of a number of letters by Jones to Watkins
reveals (as did the publication of Dylan Thomas's letters to the
same poet) the deep and serious concerns for the matter of Wales
and the craft of poetry and the deep regard the poets had for each
other. Their friendship continued to 1967, when Vernon Watkins died suddenly on a tennis court in Seattle. Watkins performed
an important service for Jones and for poetry when he arranged
and saw through to completion the first publication of Jones's
fragment "The Wall" in *Poetry*. The two poets form a pair more
suited, by outward appearances, anyway, than did Watkins and
Thomas. Both were intense, introspective, thoroughly "serious"
men; both were of the High Church, so to speak, Watkins of the
Church of England, Jones the Roman Catholic, in matters of religion and aesthetics. Watkins was the more public, more accessible
poet, whereas Jones tended to be bookish and withdrawn and devoted in a total way to art for its own sake. Watkins, for example,

wrote: "I am not saying that the need or ability to create art is the highest and most indispensable gift of man: charity is clearly that"[16] — a sentiment apparently in contradiction to Jones's insistence that man is first *homo faber*, man the artist. Both were honored in their land with degrees granted by the University of Wales; both were learned poets and men, which is to say that their learning was a matter of loves of the heart, not merely of the intellect or classical training (Watkins spent one year at Cambridge; Jones never attended any university.)

For all his mythic and Freudian concerns (see, for example, *The Ballad of the Mari Llwyd*), Watkins was preeminently a lyric poet, with a wide range of topics and a sustained output of poetry over many years. Watkins ranges farther afield, with greater variety of topics and verse forms; Jones settles in on a topic, and working at what Watkins called "glacier speed" excavates its "deposits." Both are bardic in the sense that they sing songs of praise not on behalf of one's self, and it just will not do to raise up Dylan Thomas as the epitome of things Welsh. That strutting yet vulnerable "bad boy" is no more the one authentic voice of Wales than is, say, Brendan Behan of Ireland; there is still Yeats, among a host of others, to be accounted for — that measured, senatorial voice which is often, and not by chance, the voice of Lloyds bank clerk and orthodox Anglican and Anglo-Welshman Vernon Watkins. To connect still further, this time with the war poets, Watkins noted in a review of *In Parenthesis* a "startling comparison," Jones wrote, "between some lines of Owen's *Exposure* with some lines in *In Parenthesis* about the Ypres salient. I'd never read Owen's poem, which makes the similarity extraordinary," Jones went on, and attributed the likeness to the " 'common tongue of the Zeitgeist' & partly the accidental coming together of circumstances whereby two or more persons express in almost identical forms the same thing — they may be separated by centuries & whole phases of culture."[17]

VI   *R. S. Thomas*

The letters to Vernon Watkins serve also to lead into and connect Jones with R. S. Thomas, the best-known of Wales's living poets:

Someone sent me recently a copy of some of R. S. Thomas' poems. I can't put my hand on the volume in the muddle of this damned room, but there was one I liked especially — can't recall the title — in which allusions

were made to Maelgwyn Gwynedd hiding [in] the church of Rhos fm the
Yellow Plague and other allusions, if I am not mistaken, to Dark Age
Welsh history, and as the allusions dawned on me the whole poem became
much more vital. This is a fair example of what I mean by having a
"shared background" in the *appreciation* *vis-à-vis "content" that is. D*
(it does not affect the making) of poetry.[18]

Thomas's poetry is not typically or characteristically allusive;
more often it is in a simple, direct idiom in traditional verse forms,
reminiscent of Wordsworth or the Georgians. It is a strong voice,
but without the depth of vision or demonstrated range and mastery
of word skills that Jones displays. His tone, however, is grim, bitter, sometimes to a point of cynicism, and self-critical. One reference to Arthur occurs in the brief and laconic "A Welshman to
Any Tourist":

> The hills are fine, of course,
> Bearded with water to suggest age
> And pocked with caverns,
> One being Arthur's dormitory;
> He and his knights are the bright ore
> That seams our history,
> But shame has kept them late in bed.[19]

There is a vast gap between the form and tone of expectation reso-
nant throughout Jones's "The Sleeping Lord" and Thomas's
squib. Thomas is a Welsh-speaker and vicar of a remote Welsh vil-
lage church, and perhaps the most "purely" Welsh in birth, upbringing, education, language, and chosen theme of those mentioned so far. He is the most obviously nationalist in politics in his
poetic grumbles about the English and what they have done to
Wales; more often, however, he complains even more loudly about
the Welsh natives, who have allowed themselves to be drawn away
to "the pound's climate" and have sinned by greed and complicity
in the rape of the Welsh countryside. The deposits that Jones mined
so carefully are castigated by Thomas:

> There is no present in Wales,
> And no future;
> There is only the past,
> Brittle with relics,
> Wind-bitten towers and castles
> With sham ghosts;

> Mouldering quarries and mines:
> And an impotent people,
> Sick with inbreeding,
> Worrying the carcase of an old song.[20]

In another poem, "Welsh History," he offers hope of an unspeci-
fied sort, but it is still at a far remove from such promise of a resurrection in either secular or spiritual terms as Jones posits in his
identification of Arthur with Christ as "sleeping lords" who will
reclaim their land and their own.

> We were a people, and are so yet.
> When we have finished quarrelling for crumbs
> Under the table, or gnawing the bones
> Of a dead culture, we will arise
> Armed, but not in the old way.[21]

Thomas's use of the Welsh landscape, character, and past appears
provincial in contrast to Jones. "After all," Thomas writes, "why
chant the praise of Helen, when Nest remains unsung? Why lament
Troy fallen, when Mathrafal lies in ruins?"[22] For Jones there are no
such distinctions; the deposits of Homer and Virgil are as precious
as those of the Welsh mythic past: "All must be safely gathered
in," and it is the poet's to make connections, not to splinter further
or to choose sides.

VII *Hopkins*

It is, however, the figure of Gerard Manley Hopkins, who died in
1889 but most of whose poems did not come to public attention
until they were published by Robert Bridges in 1918, who is the
closest, most important figure both for Dylan Thomas and David
Jones. This Englishman of Roman Catholic conversion and
"Welsh subscription" was to figure prominently in the work of
David Jones, who was born but six years after Hopkins's death.
Like Jones, the young Hopkins had precocious ability in drawing;
unlike Jones, he also had evident early command of language. Both
men became converts to the Roman Catholic church while in their
twenties, though with Hopkins the conversion came at a time of
intense spiritual crisis that does not have a parallel in Jones's life,
or not in any of his accounts of the event. Hopkins served in no
war, of course — no temporal war. Both poets owed much to

Wales, particularly North Wales, as in Jones's case, the source
both biographical and mythical, and in Hopkins's, the site and center of study for, their writing. Hopkins studied and learned some
Welsh and Welsh poetry while reading theology at St. Beuno's College in St. Asaph, Flintshire, and was even to write a passable
Welsh *cywydd*. But there is to be found in his English-language
poems a great deal of allusion to things Welsh, also imaginative use
of such traditional Welsh poetic devices as *cynghanedd* (q.v.), as in
"warm-laid grave of a womb-like grey" in "The Wreck of the
Deutschland." Hopkins maintained, as did Jones, that his verse
was less to be read than heard.

I have learnt Welsh, as you say: I can read easy prose and speak stumb-
lingly, but at present I find the greatest difficulty, amounting almost to
total failure, in understanding it when spoken, and the poetry, which is
quite as hard as the choruses in a Gk. play — and consider what those
would be with none but a small and bad dictionary at command — I can
make very little way with.[23]

That too was written by Hopkins, but will hold with very little
modification to describe Jones's accomplishment in the Welsh
language.
   Both poets suffered physical and nervous disabilities; both err, if
anywhere, "on the side of oddness"; [24] both put new and unaccus-
tomed strains on their readers. In his theory of poetry, his aesthetics, Hopkins drew from the Scholastic tradition and Duns
Scotus to express his ideas of individuation, inscape, instress, the
uniqueness, "this-ness," haeccity, of a thing, of a poem, and noted
"an instress and charm of Wales."[25] David Jones acknowledged
Hopkins's influence and contribution to his own thought (he read
all of Hopkins in 1928 as he was starting *In Parenthesis* — see particularly the Hopkins allusions in the titles to Parts 3 and 5). In a
letter to Vernon Watkins, Jones held that Hopkins, despite being
very Victorian in content — "though of course with the great difference of being profoundly of a Catholic mind" — did indeed
"envigorate the English language by his study of Welsh metrical
forms." He added, too, that "I may be wrong but my impression is
that Dylan T. learnt a lot fm Hopkins."[26] He was not wrong at all,
of course. The language of Hopkins's aesthetics crops up frequently in Jones's essays, particularly in his discussion of what it
means to be a "re-presentational" artist. Jones wrote too of a "certain affection for the intimate creatureliness of things — a care for,

an appreciation of the particular genius of places, men, trees, animals and yet withal a pervading sense of metamorphosis and mutability,"[27] and in a very real sense Jones's "anathemata" is a redefinition of "inscape."

Hopkins, however, was a man of intense moral and disciplined devout earnestness; he had deep reservations about the attractions of aesthetic beauty and ideals (he gave up painting when he entered the Church and was willing to renounce poetry when obliged to) that Jones evidently did not share. Jones certainly renounced self-expression in his art, but did not subject himself to self-abnegation or acute renunciation of the self. Hopkins's "I am a eunuch, but it is for the kingdom of heaven's sake"[28] could not conceivably be mistaken for a statement by Jones, nor could Hopkins's missionary zeal as expressed in: "In coming here I began to feel a desire to do something for the conversion of Wales."[29]

In his choice of poetic forms Hopkins was more versatile, but also more conservative or conventional. David Jones never attempted a sonnet of any description — at least, none was ever published — it was not a form into which he could, or chose to, wrench the grievous sense of having lost sight of God in "*A, a, a, Domine Deus.*" Both poets had a passion for precision of language, even if that meant wrenching traditional syntax, resurrecting obsolete and obscure words, and shared too a passion for all things both Welsh and Roman Catholic.

VIII *The Modernists*

To consider Hopkins is to connect and at the same time move inevitably (if but momentarily) away from the Celtic connection to the larger frame of "modernist" poetry, the most notable exemplars of whom are Eliot and Pound. Jones has certainly been noted in their company, even if snorted at as an illegitimate son of the Master. One critic wrote: "I suspect that *The Anathemata* will achieve a distinction, though a dubious one, as the very last product of the 'modern' period: it carries the method of symbolic writing, as it was prescribed some time ago by Mr. Eliot, to a final and devastating conclusion."[30] Jones is no imitator of Eliot, nor is he imitated, nor should he be, but it is important to see his place in that mode of poetry and thought which did indeed transform the map of English literature in this century.

IX   *Ezra Pound*

Jones shares with Eliot and Pound a verse style characterized by its eschewal of clear narrative continuity, and by its use of esoteric allusions, abrupt juxtapositions, relative freedom in language(s), idioms, syntax, and verse forms. But with Pound the comparison stops quickly. "Cantos" is a term far more elevated than "fragments," and there is no shortage of them. In total conception they are perhaps a far more ambitious undertaking, though to what end they point or what solution they propose is far from clear. More documentary than doctrinal, Pound has no patience to try to rescue Western civilization, the "old bitch gone in the teeth" of *Hugh Selwyn Mauberly*, from within, and there is a world of difference between the poet who idealized Mussolini and David Jones, whose vision is of a resurrected King Arthur *cum* Christ.

Canto XVI is a "war" canto, reaching beyond just the 1914–1918 War, but to quote just a few lines of it is to point the contrast in tone and method:

> And because that son of a bitch,
> > Franz Josef of Austria......
> And because that son of a bitch Napoléon Barbiche...
> They put Aldington on Hill 70, in a trench
> > dug through corpses
> With a lot of kids of sixteen,
> Howling and crying for their mamas,
> And he sent a chit back to his major:
> > I can hold out for ten minutes
> With my sergeant and a machine-gun.
> > And they rebuked him for levity.[31]

Pound goes on to touch bitterly on the war experience of Henri Gaudier, T. E. Hulme, Wyndham Lewis, and others, and like Jones alludes to other wars throughout history and the Russian revolution of 1917. But there is no sense that he sees any of it as in any way ennobling or "sacramental." Jones might well have admired Pound's techniques, though he did not read Pound until after publishing *The Anathemata* and did not write on him. He shares with Pound the practice of yoking violently together the idiom of the common man and the highly allusive esoterica of the scholar; but Jones's "low" idiom is never as low as Pound's, nor does he reach out to such diverse connections as Provençal or

China ancient and modern, or modern political causes; nor does he parade himself as did Pound. Robert Graves described Pound's verse as "sprawling, ignorant, indecent, unmelodious, seldom metrical,"[32] and while Graves is not on record with an opinion of Jones's work, it is unlikely that it would stir him to pass as severe a judgment. The fundamental difference between Jones and Pound lies, I think, in their vision, which might start from the observation that the civilization lies in ruins but proceeds in radically different ways to establish what must be preserved. For Jones, the "answer" lies wholly within the Western tradition — of monarchy, Celtic matriarchy, deep-rootedness, and Christianity; and in that context his immediate mentor is T. S. Eliot.

X   *T. S. Eliot*

I have noted elsewhere Eliot's responsibility for the first publishing of *In Parenthesis* and his "Note of Introduction" to the 1961 edition. He commented later on both *In Parenthesis* and *The Anathemata* to defend Jones (and himself) against the charge of obscurity, which is caused not by perversity, by "wilfulness or charlatanism," he noted, but by the desperate need of the artist to communicate, to share the contents of his pockets, to bring about a "surcease of solitude."[33] It is indeed an excess of solitude that is so characteristic of Eliot's early works; it is the problem of the speakers and characters in "Portrait of a Lady," "Rhapsody on a Windy Night," "The Love Song of J. Alfred Prufrock," "Preludes," and *The Waste Land*. From "Preludes" to the verse dramas *The Family Reunion* and *The Elder Statesman* is a major journey indeed, made up of a series of steps from the disguised lyric voice behind the masks of mock-Browningesque monologues to the "heap of broken images" of *The Waste Land* to the straining "I" of "Ash Wednesday" to the assured, tutorial voice of *Four Quartets*. It represents a progress that is chartable and that signifies a growth or maturing, if indeed it is not necessarily a path to be followed.

The "I" that might be the poetic voice of David Jones is scarcely ever discernible at all; and there is scarcely a discernible public "I" of David Jones that would contend with or even be acknowledged in the same context as Eliot's — the voice of the editor, reviewer, essayist, and critical sage of the century. The interrogative voice and voices of *The Waste Land* have their equivalents in *The Anathemata*, but Jones's verse does not "testify" as does Eliot's to his

conversion and its efficacy. Jones might well have suffered the twin
beasts or chimeras exemplified by "Apeneck Sweeney" and Prufrock, but they are not a part of his poetic voice, and Jones is not
concerned to exercise aloud the question, "What must I do to be
saved?" Eliot, like Pound and Odysseus, was in exile and sought a
haven; Eliot found his Penelope safe at home in the "tradition":

> So I find words I never thought to speak
> In streets I never thought I should revisit
> When I left my body on a distant shore.[34]

The *Four Quartets* are simultaneously personal and confessional
and allusive and "historic," whereas Jones rigidly eschewed the
personal pronoun "I" as if to obey, to the literal end, Eliot's
injunction in "Tradition and the Individual Talent":"Poetry is not
a turning loose of emotion, but an escape from emotion.... The
emotion of art is impersonal. And the poet cannot reach this imper-
sonality without surrendering himself wholly to the work to be
done."[35] Eliot's *Four Quartets* is a greater poem than, say, *The
Anathemata*, in that it is "a more finely perfected medium in which
special, or very varied, feelings are at liberty to enter into new
combinations."[36] I am deliberately misapplying the quotation
(Eliot is talking about the mind of a mature poet) to apply it to the
poetry, for there is a very real sense in which Jones's passion to
gather in and re-present all the deposits of the cultural past suffers
from its very disembodiment from any hint of the presence, the
"real presence," of the poet. If John Ball can exist in the present as
an extension of and embodiment of the wars of the past, why cannot he exist in a more clearly defined relationship to David Jones?
Why, in *The Anathemata*, must the mind of the poet in attendance
at the Mass be so totally severed from his bodily or emotional self?
"Tradition and the Individual Talent" does not call for total
effacement or obliteration of the self. It does not insist on its
aggrandizement, either, which is the flaw of overtly "confessional"
poetry, but surely the "I" has a mediating function. It appears in
Jones only in his prefaces and notes and occasional essays; Eliot
learned to integrate it with his meditations on the past in the poetry.
This is to point out the differences between the poets, in their most
mature, sustained works, not to insist that Jones should have "imitated" Eliot; perhaps finally it is not the autobiographical "I" so
much as a firm narrative stance or voice which serves as other than
a masked exhibitor of historical deposits that is lacking in much of
Jones's work.

XI *James Joyce*

To turn to Joyce, for whose work Jones expressed profound admiration, is to point out another contrast. There is a chartable progress in Joyce that is quite unlike Eliot's. From the miniatured realism of *Dubliners* Joyce moved to the quasi-autobiographical "new" fiction of *A Portrait of the Artist as a Young Man*. Both are lesser works than *Ulysses*, the greatness of which lies not in its baroque tapestry of interweavings of strands from Irish, Greek, Judaic, and Catholic mythologies, but from its assured sense of dealing with, both as emblems but more assuredly as living, breathing human beings, Leopold Bloom and his wife, Molly, and, to only a slightly lesser degree, Stephen Dedalus. Joyce the artist is larger than his fictional Stephen Dedalus precisely because he has that capacity for sympathetic creation. Joyce wrote *Ulysses*, Stephen Dedalus mused on "agenbite of inwit" and "the ineluctable modality of the visible." David Jones's Lady of the Pool, his "lavender girl" of Part 5 of *The Anathemata*, bears but slight resemblance to Molly Bloom; both are "literary" creations but Molly partakes literally in and is of the flesh, the Earth. Jones's *Tellus Mater*, Clio, Queen of the Woods, lavender girl, *Y Forwyn Fair*, Jill-of-the-Tump-that-Bare-Me add up to make the composite figure "The Tutelar of the Place," but she has no earthly "place" like No. 7 Eccles Street and remains an abstraction.

To note Jones's praise of Joyce is to find him praising his "carpentry" and his music and wordsmanship in "Plurabelle"; most importantly, what he admired in Joyce was that he saw him as being "of all artists ever ... the most dependent on the particular, on place, site, locality.... Never, perhaps, has such absorption with a microcosm been the means of showing forth the macrocosmic realities. He is the most incarnational of artists" (*E&A*, p. 304). Joyce was both Catholic and Celtic, like Jones; also like Jones, his medium had to be English. Those capitalized labels do not, of course, in themselves make an artist, and for Jones the perceived greatness of Joyce lay in his "proper understanding of the Catholic mind ... including both an understanding of the dogmatic and scholastic modes of thought, together with an inward understanding of a traditional, popular, rooted, vulgar, Catholic practice, sufficiently linked with the life of a land, of a *specific* countryside, and thus with the pre-Christian and immemorial thought-patterns of a genuine 'folk' " (*E&A*, p. 304). Joyce was in that sense truly a "bard," the highest praise Jones could render; he was bardic in his grasp of the knowledge of the past as much as the here and now; bardic in his passion for "the concrete, the exact dimensions, the contactual, the visual, the bodily, what the senses register" (*E&A*, p. 306); bardic in the circularity and weaving of his Celtic vision; bardic in that "Joyce has to be heard to be believed" (*E&A*, p. 307).

The "catholicity" of Joyce's mind and art is in a very real way of a greater capacity than the Roman Catholicity of Hopkins and Jones. It is of the body, and includes the comic, the brazen, the scatological, the trivial; and if the price is that Joyce might let it get away sometimes to the point of exhibitionism (in the "Oxen of the Sun" chapter in *Ulysses*, with its parading of prose styles in parody) the risk is worthwhile and to be applauded. Jones was by contrast far more self-critical and diffident, as the whole publishing history of his "fragments" in various stages of noncompletion testifies. Having once marked out the plot of ground he was to explore for further excavation and refining, Jones was the most patient and fastidious "prospector." He was that kind of loner or exile from the workaday concerns of the civilization he wished to reclaim. Both poets (the distinctions between poetry and prose being as blurred in Jones as in Joyce) were the products of those historical "accidents" which made them occupy "as it were junctional or terminal positions" in their time. Westward might indeed have been the history of the movement of money and temporal power, but Jones notes of Joyce that "it would seem providential that he did not leave 'Dear Dirty Dumpling' to go west to 'Markland's vinelands' but east in the footsteps of the great Irish scholars of the Dark Ages, to work within the boundaries of the old Roman world: that clearly was essential" (*E&A*, p. 305). Jones's spiritual odyssey took him in the same direction.

It would be quite impossible to write of Joyce that he is but quaint or antiquarian; nor will it do to dismiss David Jones. Jones lacks perhaps that truly radical energy that is so characteristic of Joyce's writings; he recognizes full well the authentic *signa* of the past, presents and re-presents them, justifies them, pleads for them. The remaining critical question is whether or not he succeeded in reinvigorating them and charging them anew with "instress." There have been few writers of this or any age so resolutely uninterested in matters of public reputation or recognition. David Jones's life work is finally his testimony to this central credo: "We were then *homo faber, homo sapiens* before Lascaux and we shall be *homo faber, homo sapiens* after the last atomic bomb has fallen" (*E&A*, p. 184).

Notes and References

(*References to David Jones's four major volumes are given in parentheses within the text and abbreviated as follows: *In Parenthesis, IP; The Anathemata, A; Epoch and Artist, E&A; The Sleeping Lord, SL.* Where the source is clear from the context, parenthetical references are to page number alone.)

Chapter One

1. Ruth Pryor, ed., *David Jones: Letters to Vernon Watkins* (Cardiff, 1976), pp. 56–57. Letter of April 11, 1962.

2. "Fragments of an Attempted Autobiographical Writing," *Agenda* (Fifteenth Anniversary Special Issue), XII:4/XIII:1 (Winter-Spring 1975), 101.

3. Letter of April 11, 1962. Pryor, *Letters*, p. 57.

4. Letter to author, August 30, 1968.

5. Letter to William T. Noon, S.J., November 7, 1965. Cited in Noon, *Poetry and Prayer* (New Brunswick, N.J., 1967), p. 338.

6. Letter of April 11, 1962. Pryor, *Letters*, p. 57.

7. "A Note to the Illustrations," *Agenda*, V:1–3 (Spring-Summer 1967), 2.

8. Letter of April 11, 1962. Pryor, *Letters*, p.. 57.

9. *Agenda*, XII:4/XIII:1 (Winter-Spring 1975), 105.

10. *Ibid.*, 106.

11. Quoted in Robin Ironside, *David Jones* (London, 1949), p. 4.

12. *Ibid.*, p. 6.

13. Letter of July, 1973, to René Hague. Quoted in Hague, *David Jones* (Cardiff, 1975), p. 50.

14. Letter to René Hague dated 27.9.74 — 11.10.74; quoted by William Blissett in Appendix A to "The Efficacious Word" in Roland Mathias, ed. *David Jones: Eight Essays on His Work as Writer and Artist* (Llandysul, 1976), p. 47.

15. *Agenda*, XII:4/XIII:1 (Winter-Spring 1975), 107.

16. Hague, *David Jones*, pp. 46–47.

17. Graves, *Goodbye to All That*, revised edition (Harmondsworth, 1957), p. 208.

18. *Agenda*, XII:4/XIII:1 (Winter-Spring 1975), 108.

19. Quoted in Richard C. Wald, " 'I Don't Think I'm Modern,' " *New York Herald Tribune Books*, July 8, 1962, p. 11.

20. Quoted in Ironside, p. 7.

21. Robert Speaight, *The Life of Eric Gill* (New York, 1966), p. 111.

22. Letter of September 13, 1921. Walter Shewring, ed., *Letters of Eric Gill* (New York, 1948), p. 148.

23. Quoted in Stanley Edgar Hyman, "T. S. Eliot and Tradition in Criticism," *The Armed Vision*, revised edition (New York, 1955), p. 70.

24. Letter of November 30, 1921. Shewring, *Letters*, p. 149.

25. Speaight, p. 105.

26. Letter to Desmond Chute, December 29, 1952. Quoted in Speaight, p. 112.

27. Quoted in Speaight, p. 149.

28. Letter of January 12, 1924. Shewring, *Letters*, p. 169.

29. Letter of May 23, 1925. Shewring, *Letters*, p. 186.

30. Quoted in John Petts, "David Jones: An Introduction," *Dock Leaves*, VI:16 (Spring 1955), 14.

31. Eric Gill, *Autobiography* (New York, 1941), p. 250.

32. Speaight, p. 227.

33. Quoted in Ben Nicholson, "Looking Back at the Thirties," *The London Magazine*, new series, V (April 1965), 47.

34. Letter of April 23, 1971 to Saunders Lewis. In *Agenda* XI:4/ XII:1 (Autumn-Winter 1973/4), 23.

35. Rayner Heppenstall, *Four Absentees* (London, 1960), p. 75.

36. Quoted in H. S. Ede, "David Jones," *Horizon*, VIII (August 1943), 128.

37. Cited from correspondence in Noon, *Poetry and Prayer*, p. 345.

38. Quoted in Wald, p. 11.

39. Letter to John H. Johnston, May 2, 1962. Cited in Johnston, *English Poetry of the First World War* (Princeton, 1964), p. 322.

40. Quoted in Wald, p. 11.

41. Read, "A Malory of the Trenches," *London Mercury*, XXVI (July 1937), 304.

42. Letter to Saunders Lewis, April 23, 1971. In *Agenda* XI:4/ XII:1 (Autumn-Winter 1973/4), 19.

43. *Ibid.*

44. *Ibid.*, p. 20.

45. Quoted in David Blamires, *David Jones: Artist and Writer* (Manchester, 1971; Toronto, 1972), pp. 10–11.

46. Quoted in Wald, p. 11.

47. Quoted in Mary Uzzell Edwards, "Genius for whom the dark is light enough," *Western Mail*, May 4, 1968.

48. Quoted in Ede, p. 131.

49. Letter to William T. Noon, November 7, 1965. Cited in Noon, *Poetry and Prayer*, p. 338.

50. Letter, "Welsh Affairs," *The Times*, March 13, 1956, p. 11.

51. Letter, "Third Programme," *The Times*, May 16, 1957, p. 13.

52. Letter to author, August 30, 1968.

53. T. S. Eliot, "Tradition and the Individual Talent," *Selected Essays*, new edition (New York, 1960), p. 6.

Chapter Two

1. Pryor, ed. *Letters*, p. 20.

2. "Introduction," *Presenting Saunders Lewis*, ed. Alun R. Jones and Gwyn Thomas (Cardiff, 1973), pp. xviii–xix.

3. Letter, "Welsh Magic," *The Times*, August 18, 1962, p. 7.

4. Goronwy Rees, "Have the Welsh a Future?" *Encounter*, XXII (March 1964), 5.

Chapter Three

1. *Agenda*, XII:4/XIII:1 (Winter-Spring 1975), 108.

2. *London Mercury*, XXVI (July 1937), 304.

3. "Comradeship Is Shared," *New York Times Book Review*, April 15, 1962, 4.

4. Quoted in Wald, pp. 3, 11.

5. *Through the Looking-Glass* (New York: Norton & Co., 1971), pp. 180–81.

Chapter Four

1. "Adam as a Welshman," *New York Review of Books*, March 1963, 12.

2. "A Note on 'In Parenthesis' and 'The Anathemata,' " *Dock Leaves*, VI:16 (Spring 1955), 21.

3. "Seven Poets and the Language," *Poetry and Fiction* (New Brunswick, N.J., 1963), p. 210.

4. Blamires, p. 195.

5. *Selected Essays*, pp. 6–7.

6. Letter to Vernon Watkins, April 11, 1962. Pryor, ed., *Letters*, pp. 60–61.

7. *Heart of Darkness* (New York, 1963), pp. 5–6.

8. *Dock Leaves*, VI:16 (Spring 1955), 22–23.

9. *A History of Welsh Literature*, trans. H. Idris Bell (London, 1955).

10. *The Burning Tree* (London, 1956), p. 15.

11. "Little Gidding," *Four Quartets*, in *Collected Poems: 1909-1962* (London, 1963), p. 222.

12. *To the Lighthouse* (New York, 1927), p. 241.

13. Encyclical Letter, *"Mediator Dei,"* November 29, 1947. Quoted in *Saint Joseph Daily Missal* (New York, 1959), p. 1.

14. *Collected Longer Poems* (London, 1968), p. 138.

Chapter Five

1. Quoted in Wald, p. 11.

2. In "Journey to Iceland," *Collected Shorter Poems: 1927-1957* (London, 1966), p. 100.

3. *The Kensington Mass* (London, 1975), p. 19.

4. See *Agenda*, XI:4/XII:1 (Autumn-Winter 1973/4), pp. 12–16.

Chapter Six

1. Paul Fussell, *The Great War and Modern Memory* (New York and London, 1975), Chapter V, p. 155.

2. *English Poetry of the First World War* (Princeton, 1964), p. 9.

3. *Agenda*, XII:4/XIII:1 (Winter-Spring 1975), 99.

4. Fussell, pp. 21–22.

5. In *Georgian Poetry*, ed. James Reeves (Harmondsworth, 1962), p. 138.

6. *The Memoirs of George Sherston* (Garden City, 1937). See *Memoirs of an Infantry Officer*, p. 148.

7. *Goodbye to All That*, p. 226.

8. *The Collected Poems of Wilfred Owen* (New York, 1964), p. 55.

9. "Prologue" to *Goodbye to All That*, revised edition (London, 1957).

10. Warren Coffey, [A review of *In Parenthesis*]. *Ramparts*, II (Autumn 1963), 90–91.

11. Thomas Parry, *A History of Welsh Literature*, trans. H. Idris Bell (London, 1955).

12. Quoted in Constantine Fitzgibbon, *The Life of Dylan Thomas* (Boston, 1965), p. 11.

13. Letter of April 29, 1955. Pryor, *Letters*, p. 22.

14. *Collected Poems* (New York, 1957), p. xv.

15. Stanza 1 of "The Forge of the Solstice," *Cypress and Acacia* (New York, 1959), p. 68.

16. "The Need of the Artist," *The Listener*, November 8, 1962, p. 757.

17. Letter of April 29, 1953. Pryor, *Letters*, p. 20.

18. Letter of April 11, 1962. Pryor, *Letters*, p. 63.

19. *Selected Poems: 1946-1968* (London, 1973), p. 41.

20. *Ibid.*, p. 9.

21. *Song at the Year's Turning* (London, 1955).

22. Quoted in R. George Thomas, "R. S. Thomas," *Andrew Young and R. S. Thomas* (London, 1964), p. 28.

23. Letter to Alexander Baillie, January 6, 1877. *Further Letters of Gerard Manley Hopkins*, ed. Claude C. Abbott (London, 1956), p. 241.

24. Letter to Robert Bridges, February 15, 1879. *The Letters of Gerard Manley Hopkins to Robert Bridges*, ed. Claude C. Abbott (London, 1935), p. 46.

25. Journal entry of September 6, 1874. *The Journals and Papers of Gerard Manley Hopkins*, ed. Humphry House (London, 1959), p. 258.

26. Letter of April 11, 1962. Pryor, *Letters*, p. 59.

27. Quoted in H. S. Ede, "David Jones," *Horizon*, VIII (August 1943), 132.

28. Letter to Robert Bridges, January 12, 1888. *The Letters . . . to Robert Bridges*, p. 270.

29. Journal entry of September 6, 1874. *The Journals . . . of Hopkins* (London, 1959), p. 258.

30. Hayden Carruth, "Poetry Chronicle: Parnassus Stormed," *Partisan Review*, XX (September-October 1953), 579.

31. *The Cantos of Ezra Pound* (New York, 1970), p. 71.

32. Quoted in G. S. Fraser, *Ezra Pound* (New York, 1960), p. 111.

33. *Dock Leaves*, VI:16 (Spring 1955), pp. 22-23.

34. "Little Gidding," *Four Quartets*, in *Collected Poems: 1909-1962* (London, 1963), p. 218.

35. *Selected Essays* (New York, 1960), pp. 10-11.

36. *Ibid.*, p. 7.

Selected Bibliography

PRIMARY SOURCES

In Parenthesis. London: Faber and Faber, 1937. Reprinted 1961 with "A Note of Introduction" by T. S. Eliot. Also New York: Chilmark Press, 1962; New York: The Viking Press (Compass Books), 1963; London: Faber and Faber, 1963, reprinted in 1969 and 1975.

The Anathemata. London: Faber and Faber, 1952; second edition, 1955. Also New York: Chilmark Press, 1963; New York: The Viking Press (Compass Books), 1965; London: Faber and Faber, 1972.

Epoch and Artist. London: Faber and Faber, 1959. Also New York: Chilmark Press, 1963; London: Faber and Faber, 1973.

The Fatigue. Cambridge: The Rampant Lions Press, 1965. Edition limited to 298 copies.

The Tribune's Visitation. London: Fulcrum Press, 1969. First edition, clothbound, limited to 150 copies; trade edition in printed wrappers.

The Sleeping Lord: and other fragments. London: Faber and Faber, 1974.

Use and Sign. Ipswich: Golgonooza Press, 1975. Edition limited to 350 copies.

The Kensington Mass. London: Agenda Editions, 1975.

David Jones: Letters to Vernon Watkins. Cardiff: University of Wales Press, 1976. Edited with Notes by Ruth Pryor; foreword by Gwen Watkins.

SECONDARY SOURCES

Agenda (David Jones Special Issue), V:1-3 (Spring-Summer 1967). Edited by William Cookson. Includes text of six poems by Jones: "*A, a, a, Domine Deus*," "The Wall," "The Dream of Private Clitus," "The Tutelar of the Place," "The Hunt," and "The Sleeping Lord"; essays, notes, and reviews by Michael Alexander, David Blamires, Louis Bonnerot, Kenneth Clark, Aneirin Talfan Davies, H. S. Ede, Nicolete Gray, René Hague, Peter Levi, Saunders Lewis, Stuart Piggott, N. K. Sandars, and Tony Stoneburner. Illustrated.

Agenda (David Jones Special Issue), XI:4/XII:1 (Autumn-Winter 1973/4). Edited by William Cookson. Includes text of "The Kensington Mass" and "The Narrows" and two letters to Saunders Lewis; essays, notes, reviews by Louis Bonnerot, William Cookson, Arthur

Giardelli, Paul Hills, John Heath-Stubbs, Nicholas Jacobs, Peter Levi, Saunders Lewis, Philip Lowery, Stuart Piggott, and N. K. Sandars. Illustrated.

Agenda (Fifteenth Anniversary Special Issue), XII:4/XIII:1 (Winter-Spring 1975). Edited by William Cookson. Includes "Fragments of an Attempted Autobiographical Writing" by Jones, and essays by René Hague and Edmund Gray.

BERGONZI, BERNARD. *Heroes' Twilight: A Study of the Literature of the Great War.* London: Constable; New York: Coward-McCann, 1965. See Chapter 10, "Remythologizing," pp. 198-212. A wide-ranging discussion of Jones in the context of the literature of the 1914-1918 War that tests the possibility of "epic" poetry in an age seen as not given to "the rhetoric and gestures of heroism"

BLAMIRES, DAVID. *David Jones: Artist and Writer.* Manchester: Manchester University Press, 1971; Toronto: University of Toronto Press, 1972. A major full-length study of Jones that includes biography, extended consideration of Jones as visual artist, and detailed studies of the published writings to 1971. Illustrated.

BLISSETT, WILLIAM F. "David Jones: 'Himself at the Cavemouth,' " *University of Toronto Quarterly,* XXXVI:3 (April 1967), 259-273. A detailed textual study of the cave imagery in *The Anathemata.*

_____. "*In Parenthesis* Among the War Books," *University of Toronto Quarterly,* XLII:3 (Spring 1973), 258-88. A closely detailed study of *In Parenthesis* in comparison to other books of prose and poetry treating the 1914-1918 War; includes extensive notes "that may be useful to students of war literature in general."

BONNEROT, LOUIS. "*The Anathemata* de David Jones: Poème Epique et Eucharistique." *Etudes Anglaises,* XXIV:3 (Juillet-Septembre 1971), 233-56. In French, a major critical study of *The Anathemata* and its construction, seen in the context of the poetry of Eliot, Joyce, Hopkins, Pound.

_____. "David Jones, Poète du Sacré." *Etudes* (Avril 1973), 575-88. In French, a substantial essay touching on most of Jones's work and ideas with particular attention to the relationship of the arts visual and written.

CLEVERDON, DOUGLAS. *Word and Image IV: David Jones, b. 1895.* London: The National Book League, 1972. Catalogue for an exhibition of Jones's paintings, engravings, and writings; well illustrated and annotated with reference to letters, manuscripts, broadcasts.

Dock Leaves (A David Jones Number), VI:16 (Spring 1955). Edited by Raymond Garlick. Includes essay "History and Pre-History" by David Jones; essays by T. S. Eliot, Saunders Lewis, and John Petts.

FUSSELL, PAUL. *The Great War and Modern Memory.* New York and London: Oxford University Press, 1975. A major study of the literature, both "serious" and otherwise, of the war, with frequent attention to Jones — see section, "The Honorable Miscarriage of *In Parenthesis*," pp. 144–54.

HAGUE, RENÉ. *A Commentary on The Anathemata of David Jones*. Wellingborough, England: Christopher Skelton, 1977. A line-by-line, section-by-section elucidation of *The Anathemata,* its allusions, references, and sources. An indispensable guide by one who knew Jones intimately for fifty years, amply documented from Hague's private conversations and correspondence with the poet.

_____. *David Jones*. Cardiff: The University of Wales Press and the Welsh Arts Council (Writers of Wales Series), 1975. Of major interest and importance because of the biographical connections between Hague and Jones; includes substantial quotation from correspondence. More a personal tribute than a conventional scholarly work.

HOOKER, JEREMY. *David Jones: An Exploratory Study of the Writings*. London: Enitharmon Press, 1975. An extended monograph of close critical study of *In Parenthesis* and *The Anathemata* and the "fragments."

IRONSIDE, ROBIN. *David Jones*. Hardmondsworth: Penguin Books (Modern Painters Series), 1949. A critical description of Jones's paintings which includes some biography; well illustrated with 16 color, 16 black-and-white plates.

JOHNSTON, JOHN H. *English Poetry of the First World War*. London: Oxford University Press; Princeton: Princeton University Press, 1964. A study of ten soldier-poets of the 1914-1918 War; see Chapter VIII, pp. 284–340. *In Parenthesis* is seen as "an original work which testifies to the perennial power of poetry to adapt itself to new circumstances and to renew its vitality through the processes of that adaptation."

KERMODE, FRANK. *Puzzles and Epiphanies: Essays and Reviews, 1958-1961*. London: Routledge and Kegan, 1962. See Chapter II, pp. 29–34. Originally a review of *Epoch and Artist*.

LEVI, PETER, S.J. *In Memory of David Jones*. London: The Tablet, 1975. The text of a sermon delivered in Westminster Cathedral at the Solemn Requiem held for David Jones on December 13, 1974.

MATHIAS, ROLAND. Editor, *David Jones: Eight Essays on His Work as Writer and Artist*. Llandysul: Gomer Press, 1976. Essays by David Blamires, William F. Blissett, Arthur Giardelli, Désirée Hirst, Jeremy Hooker, Peter Orr, and N. K. Sandars, first given as lectures at the David Jones Weekend Conference of *Yr Academi Gymreig*, Aberystwyth, Wales, in September 1975.

NOON, WILLIAM T., S.J. *Poetry and Prayer*. New Brunswick, N.J.: Rutgers University Press, 1967. Chapter 8, pp. 225–59, is a study of *The Anathemata* in a book that examines Jones in the context of, primarily, Hopkins, Yeats, Wallace Stevens, and Robert Frost.

ORR, PETER. Editor, *The Poet Speaks: Interviews with Contemporary*

Poets. London: Routledge and Kegan Paul, 1966. Includes the text of an interview with Jones recorded on November 24, 1964.

Poetry Wales (A David Jones Number), VIII:3 (Winter 1972). Edited by Meic Stephens. Includes a letter by David Jones; essays, notes, reviews by Douglas Cleverdon, Pennar Davies, Arthur Giardelli, Désirée Hirst, Jeremy Hooker, Mary E. Jones, Saunders Lewis, Alun Llewellyn-Williams, D. Tecwyn Lloyd, J. E. Meredith, Philip Pacey, and Gwyn Williams. Illustrated.

RAINE, KATHLEEN. *David Jones: Solitary Perfectionist.* Ipswich: Golgonooza Press, 1974–75. Enlarged to three chapters from a 1974 limited edition; high praise of Jones as "the last English writer of great genius who wrote as a living member of European Christendom."

REES, SAMUEL. *David Jones: An Annotated Bibliography and Guide to Research.* New York and London: Garland Publishing, 1977. Includes listing of Jones's works in prose and poetry; bibliography of writings about him in books, theses, journals, newspapers, etc.; listing of broadcasts and notes on current research.

ROSENBERG, HAROLD. "Aesthetics of Crisis," *The New Yorker,* August 22, 1964, pp. 114–22. A substantial review of *Epoch and Artist,* which Jones described as "the only proper criticism of that heterogeneous collection of stuff."

SILKIN, JON. *Out of Battle: The Poetry of the Great War.* London: Oxford University Press, 1972. Includes a chapter on David Jones among the war poets and raises some questions about Jones's attempt at epic-making and the concomitant moral ambiguities.

SPEARS, MONROE K. "Shapes and Surfaces: David Jones, with a Glance at Charles Tomlinson," *Contemporary Literature,* XII:4 (Autumn 1971), 402–19.

WHITE, GEORGE ABBOTT, and NEWMAN, CHARLES. Editors, *Literature in Revolution.* New York: Holt, Rinehart and Winston (Tri-Quarterly Book), 1972. See Charles J. (Tony) Stoneburner, "Notes on Prophecy and Apocalypse in a Time of Anarchy and Revolution: A Trying Out," pp. 246–82.

Index

Aeneid, The (Virgil), 82

Amis, Kingsley, 128

Anabasis (St. John Perse), 27

"Andrea del Sarto" (Browning), 120

Aneirin, 52, 54, 126, 130

Arthur, 13, 25, 37-41, 44, 64, 70, 85, 88, 90, 100, 111-15, 118-20, 123, 132, 133, 136

"Ash Wednesday" (Eliot), 92, 137

Auden, W. H., 30, 75, 97, 105, 106, 120

"Author's Prologue" (D. Thomas), 129

Ballad ri Llwyd, The (Watkins), 131

Bayes, Walter, 18

Behan, Brendan, 131

Bell, Sir H. Idris, 128

Blake, William, 19, 37, 94

Blunden, Edmund, 122, 126

Borrow, George, 54

Bradshaw, Ebenezer, 13, 21, 84, 93

Bridges, Robert, 133

Brooke, Rupert, 66, 122-24

Browning, Robert, 54, 106, 120

"Bugler's First Communion, The" (Hopkins), 60

Blamires, David, 76

Bunyan, John, 14, 54

Byron, George Gordon (Lord), 127

Cantos, The (Pound), 121, 136

"Carpenter's Son, The" (Housman), 106

Carroll, Lewis, 54, 64, 68

"Charge of the Light Brigade, The" (Tennyson), 123

Chaucer, Geoffrey, 26, 37, 54

Chester Play of the Deluge, The, 22

Chesterton, G. K., 19

"Child's Christmas in Wales, A" (D. Thomas), 129

Chute, Father Desmond, 20, 22, 27

"Cleon" (Browning), 106, 120

Coffey, Warren, 128

Coleridge, Samuel Taylor, 54, 56, 85, 95

Conrad, Joseph, 83-84, 122

Crehan, Father, 43

"*Culwch ac Olwen*", 39, 112, 126

cynghanedd, 89, 134

D'Arcy, Martin C. (S.J.), 24

Dawson, Christopher, 25-26

"Dead Boche" (Graves), 124

"Destruction of Sennacherib, The" (Byron), 127

Drayton, Michael, 37

"Dream of the Rood, The", 91

Dubliners (Joyce), 139

"Dulce et Decorum Est" (Owen), 124

Dunbar, William, 54, 62

Duns Scotus, 134

Ede, H. S., 31

Elder Statesman, The (Eliot), 137

Eliot, T. S., 20, 25-27, 32, 41, 49, 51, 76, 78, 87, 90, 92, 106, 120-22, 135-38

Elizabeth II, 41-43

Ennius, 23

"Epistle . . . Karshish, An" (Browning), 106

Evans, Caradoc, 130

"Exposure," (Owen), 131

Ezekiel, 125

Family Reunion, The (Eliot), 137

Farewell to Arms, A (Hemingway), 127

"Fern Hill" (D. Thomas), 129

Finnegans Wake (Joyce), 27, 89-90, 139

For the Time Being (Auden), 97, 106

Ford, Ford Madox (Hueffer), 122

Forster, E. M., 122

Four Quartets (Eliot), 90, 137-38

"Fra Lippo Lippi" (Browning), 120

Frazer, Sir James G., 26
From Ritual to Romance (Weston),26
Fussell, Paul, 124

Gaudier, Henri, 136
Gauguin, Paul, 15
Geoffrey of Monmouth, 37, 39-40
Gibbings, Robert, 22
Gill, Eric, 11, 18-24, 27, 34
Glyn Dŵr, Owain, 41
Gododdin, y (Aneirin), 52, 90, 119, 126, 130
Golden Bough, The (Frazer), 26
Goodbye to All That (Graves), 126
Graves, Robert, 16-18, 122, 124, 126-27, 137
Grenfell, Julian, 122-23
Grisewood, Harman, 30
Gulliver's Travels (Swift), 21
Gwilym, Dafydd ap, 130
Gwynne-Williams, Valerie, 41

Hague, René, 16, 23, 118
Hardy, Thomas, 122
Hartrick, A. S., 15
Heart of Darkness (Conrad), 83
Hector, 82, 90-91, 116, 123
Helen (of Troy), 85, 133
Hemingway, Ernest, 127
Henry V, 64
Henry V (Shakespeare), 58-59, 116
Henry VII, 123
Henry VIII, 123
Hepworth, Barbara, 24
Herbert, George, 128
Historia Regum Brittaniae (Geoffrey of Monmouth), 39
Homer, 64, 126-27, 133
Hopkins, Gerard Manley, 20, 25, 27, 42, 54, 60-61, 64, 101, 121, 127, 130, 133-35, 140
Housman, A. E., 106
How Green Was My Valley (R. Llewellyn), 89
"Hugh Selwyn Mauberley" (Pound), 136
Hulme, T. E., 136
Hunting of the Snark, The (Carroll), 68
Hutchens, Ivon, 23

I, Claudius (Graves), 127

Idylls of the King, The (Tennyson), 38, 123
Iliad, The (Homer), 116
Isaiah, 82, 90, 91

Johnston, John H., 122
Jonah, 22
Jones, David (1895-1974), and Anglo-Welsh poetry, 121, 128-35; and modernist writers, 121, 135-41; and poets of 1914-1918 War, 121-28; as an art student, 11, 15, 18, 20-21; as painter and engraver, 18-26, 28, 36; beginnings as a writer, 26, 49; connection with Eric Gill, 11, 19-21; conversion to Roman Catholicism, 11-12, 18-23, 47; death, 31; early life, 12-15; family background, 12-15; later years, 29-33; literary prizes and honors, 27, 30; middle years, 27-29; nervous disorders, 18, 23, 26, 28, 127; service in 1914-1918 War, 11-12, 15-18, 121, 138; Welsh ancestry, 11-14, 20, 128, 133-34; Welsh language, 14, 32, 132, 134; wounding in 1914-1918 War, 16-17

WORKS-POETRY:
Anathemata, The, 13, 14, 23, 25, 28-30, 34-36, 42, 47, *74-98*, 104, 113-15, 118-19, 135-39
In Parenthesis, 12-13, 16-20, 26-31, 34-36, *49-73*, 79-80, 90, 97, 99-100, 102, 104, 115, 117-19, 121-23, 125-27, 129, 131, 134, 137-38
Sleeping Lord, The, 30-31, *99-120*: "A, a, a, Domine Deus," 28, 48, 99-101, 135; "Book of Balaam's Ass, The," 99, 115-18; "Dream of Private Clitus, The," 31, 99, 103-105, 116; "Fatigue, The," 31, 99, 105-107, 116, 118; "Hunt, The," 39, 100, 112-13, 120; "Sleeping Lord, The," 39, 100, 113-15; "Tribune's Visitation, The," 31, 99, 107-109, 120; "Tutelar of the Place, The," 31, 99, 109-111, 116, 120, 127, 139; "Wall, The," 30, 99, 101-103, 130
Other poems: "Kensington Mass, The," 118-19; "Narrows, The," 119-20

Paintings and engravings, 15, 21-25, 28, 31

Prose
Epoch and Artist, 30, *34-48*, 100: "Art and Sacrament," 20, 37, 44-48, 76; "Autobiographical Talk," 12-14, 18, 22; "James Joyce's Dublin," 139-40; "Myth of Arthur, The," 37-41, 76; "Preface," 11-12; "Wales and the Crown," 37, 40-44; "Utile, The," 141

"Journey of the Magi, The" (Eliot), 106

Joyce, James, 25, 34, 51, 78, 89, 90, 121-22, 139-40

Kenner, Hugh, 30
King Lear (Shakespeare), 88
Kipling, Rudyard, 54, 122
Knight, W. F. Jackson, 30

Lady Chatterley's Lover (Lawrence), 21
"Lament for the Makaris" (Dunbar), 62
Lawrence, D. H., 122
Lays of Ancient Rome (Macaulay), 13
Lewis, Saunders, 41
Lewis, Wyndham, 136
Llywelyn ap Gruffydd, 40, 43, 113, 115, 123
"Locksley Hall" (Tennyson), 123
"Love Song of J. Alfred Prufrock, The" (Eliot), 137-38

Mabinogion, The, 39, 54, 91, 112, 130
Macbeth (Shakespeare), 85
Malory, Sir Thomas, 26-27, 37-40, 54, 62, 64, 66, 73, 91, 127
Mandeville, Sir John, 52
Maritain, Jacques, 22, 25
Masefield, John, 122
Maud (Tennyson), 123
Maxwell, George, 21
Memoirs of a Fox-Hunting Man (Sassoon), 126
Memoirs of an Infantry Officer (Sassoon), 126
Meninsky, Bernard, 18
Milton, John, 27, 37-38, 97

Moore, Henry, 24
Morris, William, 124
Morte Darthur (Malory), 38-40
Muir, Edwin, 30
Mussolini, 136

Nemerov, Howard, 30, 76
Nennius, 37
Newman, John Henry Cardinal, 61
Nicholson, Ben, 23
Nicholson, Nancy, 127
"Note of Introduction, A" (Eliot), 51, 121, 137

O'Connor, Father John, 19, 118
Odyssey, The (Homer), 89
"On Being Asked for a War Poem" (Yeats), 55
Owen, Wilfred, 122, 124-26, 131

Parry, Sir Thomas, 89
Pepler, Hilary, 21, 27
Pius XII, Pope, 93
Plaid Cymru, 41
Pope, Alexander, 127
"Portrait of a Lady" (Eliot), 137
Portrait of the Artist as a Young Man, A (Joyce), 139
Pound, Ezra, 51, 121-22, 135-37
"Preludes" (Eliot), 137

Raine, Kathleen, 30
Read, Herbert, 27, 49, 122
Resurrection, The (Yeats), 106
"Rhapsody on a Windy Night" (Eliot), 137
"Rime of the Ancient Mariner, The" (Coleridge), 21, 56, 85, 95
Rosenberg, Isaac, 122

St. Luke (Gospel of), 77
St. Paul, 20, 109
Sassoon, Siegfried, 16, 122, 124, 126
Savage, Reginald, 15
"Second Coming, The" (Yeats), 111
Shakespeare, William, 27, 54, 58, 64, 116
Shelley, Percy B., 80
Smart, Christopher, 34
Song of Roland, The, 66, 119

Sorley, Charles, 122
Spender, Stephen, 49
Spenser, Edmund, 37-38
Stevens, Wallace, 98
Sutherland, Helen, 23-24

Taliesin, 91
Tennyson, Alfred Lord, 37-38, 54, 123-24, 127
Thomas, Dylan, 31, 92, 121, 129, 131, 133-34
Thomas, Edward, 122
Thomas, R. S., 121, 131-32
To the Lighthouse (Woolf), 90
"Tradition and the Individual Talent" (Eliot), 33, 138

Ulysses (Joyce), 89, 139-40
Under Milkwood (D. Thomas), 92, 129
Undertones of War (Blunden), 126

Vaughan, Henry, 128

Virgil, 23, 82, 85, 90-91, 127, 133
Vision, A (Yeats), 111

Waste Land, The (Eliot), 26-27, 90, 137
Watkins, Vernon, 15, 35, 80, 101, 109, 121, 130-31, 134
Wells, H. G., 66
"Welsh History" (R. S. Thomas), 133
"Welshman to any Tourist, A" (R. S. Thomas), 133
Weston, Jessie L., 26
White Goddess, The (Graves), 127
Wilde, Oscar, 98
Williams, Charles, 37
Williams, Gwyn, 89
Williams, Sir Ifor, 51
Woolf, Virginia, 90, 122
Wordsworth, William, 127, 132
"Wreck of the Deutschland, The" (Hopkins), 134

Yeats, W. B., 55, 97, 106, 111, 120, 122, 131